I LO[...]
YOUR ENCOURAGEMENT
& WISDOM THIS BOOK
MAY NEVER HAVE BEEN,

(WITH LOVE)

THE CONSCIOUS OMNIVERSE

RECEIVED THROUGH DIRECT TRANCE COMMUNICATION BY DAVID WATSON
TRANSCRIPTS AND ADAPTATION BY G. C. SMITH

Bloomington, IN  Milton Keynes, UK

AuthorHouse™
1663 Liberty Drive, Suite 200
Bloomington, IN 47403
www.authorhouse.com
Phone: 1-800-839-8640

AuthorHouse™ UK Ltd.
500 Avebury Boulevard
Central Milton Keynes, MK9 2BE
www.authorhouse.co.uk
Phone: 08001974150

This book is a work of non-fiction. Unless otherwise noted, the author and the publisher make no explicit guarantees as to the accuracy of the information contained in this book and in some cases, names of people and places have been altered to protect their privacy.

© *2006 TRANSCRIPTS AND ADAPTATION BY G. C. SMITH. All rights reserved.*

No part of this book may be reproduced, stored in a retrieval system, or transmitted by any means without the written permission of the author.

First published by AuthorHouse 4/25/2006

ISBN: 1-4184-7817-2 (sc)

Printed in the United States of America
Bloomington, Indiana

This book is printed on acid-free paper.

Acknowledgements and special thanks to:

Marni Swihart - Trance Director

Isauro A. Salas Alfonso - Artwork

TABLE OF CONTENTS

- 1 - GOD 1
- 2 - DEATH 12
- 3 - SOUL 33
- 4 - NON-PHYSICALS 74
- 5 - EXTRATERRESTRIALS 86
- 6 - APPENDIX 120
- 7 - SOME AFTERTHOUGHTS FROM THE WILLOWS 134

FOREWORD

We, of The Willows, greet you dear reader, and suggest that it is your present state of understanding which has brought you to this particular publication. It has been your own thoughts and personal inclinations which have caused you to pick up this book. As you are reading these very words in front of you, it is important to realise that you are already connecting with the energy of which we are a part, and you are a part - the energy of the oneness of all existence.

As well, it is imperative for us to state that The Willows are not divine teachers. We are merely a reflection of your own inner knowingness. As you are reading our words, which have been spoken through, and transcribed by our physical connections and nexus points David Watson and G.C. Smith, it will reflect your own inner awareness and being. Once these words have been ingested and the meanings externalised, the presentation and format will provide an opportunity to truly stimulate that part of you which is also a part of the greater whole.

We welcome you to your world, to our world, and to the new world, because from this time forward, a new world is opening within each and every magical moment.

With love and respect from us to you,

The Willows

A GREETING FROM DAVID WATSON

When G. C. Smith and I began our discussions about writing this book in conjunction with The Willows, I was very hesitant. After all, so much brilliant information has been channelled by so many others in recent years, that I couldn't see any point in reinventing the wheel. Yet, the more I thought about it, the more I realized that I have chosen to channel. The Willows have much to offer all of us, and if similar information has been provided by other sources, then all the better. The Willows represent one more reflection of an eternal mystery. They enter our world by invitation, helping us to discover the reasons why things are.

There is no adequate definition to explain channelling. Each of us who works with spirit, energy, qui, chi or prana, have our own stories and visions of what we do, and also, what all of this might be about - and so do you!

You are you, existing as an infinite creation encapsulated within each single moment. Within that same moment, you are channelling yourself, because you are your consciousness, and that very consciousness creates you. I believe that the purpose of consciousness is to know more, and to become more aware, because awareness brings understanding, and with that understanding comes love. So, in essence, the road to channelling is opening oneself to that from which we are created, while at the same time, inviting that source to flow through us with truth and love.

Many of us have tried to make sense of this thing we call existence, and the life experience which accompanies it. Thinking about this book, *The Conscious Omniverse*, my hope is that while you are reading these words, perhaps something of what The Willows have to say will resonate somewhere deep within, and connect with your own unique view of the world. So read, process and enjoy, and do share your thoughts with us about this book.

Respectfully,
David

TESTIMONIAL FROM MARNIE SWIHART

For the past several years, I have acted as David's director as he channels The Willows. It is my responsibility to ensure that a smooth and productive session takes place for each of his clients. Over a period of time, I began to notice a particular pattern forming as clients posed their questions to The Willows. Even today, those who come to David to connect with The Willows, express a distinct desire to become more than what they presently perceive themselves to be. Deep within, these individuals hold certain knowledge that somehow, there's more to this life than what they have been taught. Subsequently, they seek to discover and connect with their origins and that state which preceded physical birth. Many questioners will focus on the validity of a God or a Supreme Being, the purpose of their lives, or how they might connect with the Life Force. Hopefully, this book will shed some light into many of these areas.

Like yourselves, David Watson, G. C. Smith and I, are seekers on the path for personal truth, and it is our wish that this enquiry into the nature of being will provide you with some of the information that you require at this stage of your journey.

INTRODUCTION

The following information provided by The Willows, attempts to transfer concepts and images for which there are neither suitable words, nor adequate representations which fit into our current perceptual models of reality and third dimensional thinking. For those who persevere with these writings in their entirety, The Willows suggest that each reader should begin to glean one's own individual truth, if any, from what has been given.

The Willows state that there exists but one soul, or sole consciousness, which is shared throughout all of creation. What many think of as God, The Totality, or That Which Is, is neither a separate entity, nor does it possess a consciousness which is segregated from its parts. It is the parts, such as ourselves, which possess self-consciousness, and it is this differentiation which creates the awareness of a whole.

As a result of misunderstanding this state of affairs, humankind tends to project its own images of either a personal or impersonal God, a supreme being with an ego, and thereby, creates an imaginary entity responsible for creation, and yet, separate from it. By such practices, mankind has failed to realize that it is the consciousness of the parts themselves, or ourselves, which engenders this awareness of a whole, because it is only through individuation that there can be an acknowledgment of another consciousness in the first place.

The Willows strive constantly to demonstrate the connectivity of all conscious and sentient life. One of the main propositions that The Willows have put forward, is that to experience the awareness of an independent self, such as a human life, a separation from The Totality must occur. To experience a self-conscious existence, some form of differentiation is required which will allow for a perceiver to acknowledge itself as separate and apart from what is being perceived.

The Willows proclaim that there is a creative energy, or spirit, which is universal, and fuels everything which exists. In itself, this spirit has no self-directed or individualized consciousness, that is, an awareness of self in a subjective sense which stands apart from its creations. Paradoxically, it is this original creative force which provides self-conscious actualization for a myriad of innumerable life forms, both sentient and non-sentient. Therefore, to envision The Totality or That Which Is, the reader might wish to conceptualize a collective consciousness, rather than a singular conscious entity which humanity envisions as a separate, all-knowing entity called God.

The idea of a unified consciousness, or an omniscient God who remains outside of creation, is not going to disappear totally from our belief systems at this point in human evolution. Due to the current way in which humanity perceives its existence, and the manner in which it processes information, the idea of a subjective God, or an all-knowing being who possesses an absolute consciousness, will continue to be an arguable concept.

The Willows insist that spirit energy, or the creative force of existence, is a prerequisite to all life, not only in the physical, but throughout all of creation. This energy which maintains the cosmos is not self-conscious, even though it permeates All Which Is. Self-consciousness can only arise through the individuation of this energy into countless life forms, a process which will continue into infinity, in all dimensions, all spaces, and throughout all times.

All of us, here and now, who are physically conscious in this moment exist as one of the offshoots of this dispersed energy. We are it, and it is us. Even though every self-aware being experiences its self-consciousness as apart from the whole, at the same time, all are contained within That Which Is. In this sense, we are God, and as such, exist as minute components within that oneness. In reality, there is no differentiation amongst anything in creation. Divisions are created by self-awareness, the capacity to experience a separate identity by individuating from the whole.

It is our own thoughts, beliefs, and imaginings, which give rise to an all-powerful, self conscious, and self-willed being, a God who is above and beyond us and the controller of the universe. According to The Willows, it is only humankind which harbours such distinctions regarding a greater or lesser beingness. By imagining a supreme being to whom each person is accountable, humanity, of all the higher intelligent life forms inhabiting the physical universe is the only species which diminishes itself by subjugating its existence to an omniscient, self-conscious superior being. The Willows are not suggesting that we embrace a philosophy of agnosticism, atheism or nihilism, but merely pointing out that the search for the origins of consciousness should begin within each individual's very own self, because within each individuated life form resides That Which Is.

One of the greatest difficulties that The Willows encounter is the attempt to describe immateriality to material beings because our terminology and reference points are almost exclusively based in physicality. There are few words in human languages which define or describe states of consciousness which are not founded upon a sentient experience of reality. Our physical actuality is a perceptual one. It is grounded in information received by the five senses. Data, which is processed by a physical brain and nervous system, provides the substance for our conceptualizations, and it is through that commonality of physical experience that we communicate through spoken and written languages.

To comprehend a non-physical state of being, no word referents exist which could even begin to convey a non-material mode of existence in terms which would be comprehensible to our present understanding. The Willows have attempted in a variety of ways to provide glimpses of non-corporeal reality by adopting the only tools available - humanity's own vague terms of reference for non-physicality. This is complicated further because words such as soul or spirit have different meanings in the ways they are used and understood by various belief systems and religions.

Consciousness beyond the third dimension is radically different to what we experience here on the physical plane. The Willows caution the reader to be aware that an entity, whose sole reality is derived from a human state of consciousness, would have to join them and enter fully into their realms of existence to comprehend their state of being. Throughout this book, The Willows have provided several key exercises to assist readers in releasing their consciousness from its hold on the physical. When all is said and done, however, The Willows point out that the proof of the pudding is in the eating, and therefore, words can never replace direct experience.

G. C. Smith

- 1 -

GOD

Would you provide us with your comments on the creative process and the God concept?

We will do it in a sense which will allow you to understand how the concept of God works. God is a separate vision for each individual upon the physical plane. There are different understandings of what God is, and who God is. It depends on an individual's upbringing, family interactions, religious beliefs, and openness of mind, all of which determine how the idea of a creative energy known as God will inevitably develop, even for those who declare themselves to be neutral or agnostic. It's important to understand that the very experience of consciousness which accompanies existence on your plane, involves a creative energy to produce this interactive situation of man and God.

Understand that God is always a reflection of the individual, and therefore, not only a concept of religion. Many religions have declared the specifics of God, and some of that specificity includes physical descriptions. Due to the beliefs of the Hindus, they will describe what Vishnu, Krishna, and Brahman look like, and also provide you with pictures. Christianity - and in particular progressive Christians - has produced drawings depicting Christ, the one who is thought to have been a manifestation of God in the physical.

Alternatively, within the original beliefs of Judaism, there have been no images offered. God is considered to be an energy form, comprised of the totality of existence. The Judaic view fell into step with many other similar visions which suggested that God is creative energy.

To gain a fuller concept of God by examining just one particular viewpoint would confuse every individual reading this book. We can, however, provide you with a model which might be of benefit to you. If you choose to contemplate what we are about to present, you can determine if similarities exist which correspond to your own beliefs about God, and by doing so, you will understand that God is more than just power.

God is given credence by those on your plane who envision life as an on-going process. The concept of a God has emerged from the idea that creation encompasses everything which exists. In the distant past, those who considered that God must be conscious developed a further concept which suggested a need for this being to manifest physically, outside of its spiritual or energetic base. This idea provided the basis for the creationist viewpoint, a belief that there had to be a beginning to God, but that this God also remained outside of time and space. Such a God, however, was neither assigned precise dimensions, nor given a true description which could be interpreted and understood by a mind conditioned to view reality from within the third dimension.

That being said, humanity still requires some comprehension of its source, and therefore, seeks knowledge of a progenitor of life, but as mankind understands it, that source is unknowable. Do realize that the concept of a God is not necessarily a universal need, but one which is unique to the earth and to humankind in general. As humanity projects its concept of a God beyond the earth and into other aspects of the universe, countless visions arise regarding creation and the original energy attached to it. Therefore, each individual's personal projections and conceptualizations of a God will always lack a cohesive or universal validity.

The energy of creation is eternal and infinite. It's original, and it can never be anything else but original. In fact, it's the tapestry and the canvas for all physical existence. In some aboriginal cultures, including the indigenous people of North America, this is referred to as the Great Mystery. Contained within that Great Mystery is the energy of the Great Spirit, which serves as a representation of the energy involved in the creative processes which occur on the physical plane, including evolution.

Similarly, in the beliefs of Catholicism, there is a Father, a Son, and a Holy Ghost. The Son represents that which has come from the infinity of the Father, or the creative energy and the original Great Mystery, but the Son, can also be viewed as the Great Spirit as well. The Holy Ghost represents the spirit of all, which animates on your plane of consciousness. So all three of these energies serve as representations of creation.

Although each person's view of God differs from another, you cannot ignore the fact that you exist and that you hold within yourself the gifts of both awareness and self-awareness, along with the ability to interrelate with the environment where you exist. This provides you with an opportunity not only to move forward in life, but also to create waves.

As far as establishing a conceptual basis for God, it's not possible to pin God down to the ultimate of ultimates. When attempting to understand an all-inclusive supreme being, there can be only a consideration of the various elements which comprise one's conceptual overview. So when you contemplate what you understand to be God, first, you must begin with yourself as an individual. You need to realise that due to the fact that you exist, you must be a reflection of that supreme energy, and therefore, you cannot be separate from your original source.

With this concept in mind, it's important for readers to consider themselves as God. We make no bones about this, because every entity is a reflection of the original creative energy. Subsequently, by that very definition, all must be God, and yet, in contrast, most entities feel and hold themselves as being below that process of ultimate creation. This is because they have not learned to integrate themselves, and have not understood the importance of viewing themselves as existing independently of the creative energy, while simultaneously, remaining part of it. This gives rise to an interesting set of circumstances, if indeed, any of it can be consciously comprehended.

To give you a basic overview of God, we will say that it's an energetic continuation of creation, a process which is constantly changing and evolving. This God, is both the life force and the life forms, and this energy invades and percolates in every cell in your body and every cell of every other body. Understand that no matter how large or how small, this energy is shared amongst all sentients on all levels of consciousness, and it provides a wide spectrum of interchange. This allows all individuals the opportunity to determine what God means to them, personally, through their own observations of the world. For God is always a reflection of one's own individual consciousness.

So is God just a concept of each individual?

To answer your question which refers to the conceptualisation of God, you are correct in assuming that God means something different to each person. In this way, it is necessary to understand that our use of the word God is not used as a noun, but as a verb, because creation and God are synonymous.

It is important for people to understand that this is an active aspect of the term God, and is synonymous with creation. That Which Is, is in a constant state of unfolding and becoming. That is God. It is important that people understand God in this active sense. God is a word which is non-specific. No one can draw a picture of God on which everyone would agree. No one can show you God in a bottle, so that everyone might look and say: *This is God - is it not?* Therefore, understand that the terminology as we have applied it, means that God is That Which Is, which includes both the living and non-living aspects of your physical world. This is indeed, what God is - That Which Is. God is That Which Is, the constant state of existence. It unfolds continuously through a creative effort, and expands by the manner in which it exists. This is the only way it can be understood.

Was there a Big Bang and a singular moment of creation?

Humanity maintains a current understanding that there was a beginning to the universe. Your scientists have referred to it as the Big Bang of creation. We have called it the big bop or pop. Whether it be pop, bop or bang, it's irrelevant. There was no such beginning. We would like to point out that what your science takes into account, has been derived from physical knowledge only. Although many of you have been conditioned by others into adopting certain belief systems, your concepts of the universe have been formulated and acquired over a very short period of time. Those claiming expertise in all things concerning physical matter, are but novices when one compares the last few hundred years of your scientific history to the timelessness of creation.

The information gathered by the scientific community of the earth, has been based on observation and experimentation. When it comes to discussing matters which are outside of the physical sphere or things which are related to the vast expanse of time, then theorising is the only methodology by which conclusions can be reached. Mankind's vision of existence does not go beyond one's personal birth, a short lifespan, and one's inevitable demise, and therefore, certain limitations are inherent within your scientific process.

So what you are attempting to accomplish from your own viewpoint concerning existence, is to transfer your human observations onto the universe in the form of a birth, expansion and death. It's as if God, Vishnu, Krishna, or the Great Mystery, could be born, live, and then die. It's not like that in any sense, for you must understand that the initial explosion which has been theorized by many of today's physicists is simply a theory. There is much which is being explored in quantum physics, which is beginning to move away from such a singular understanding that there had to be one, absolute creative moment.

Many of you have been conditioned by others into adopting certain belief systems. Do understand though, that if there could be such a thing as one single creative instant, such an event would occur at the point when each inner awareness began its existence. That one flash into consciousness is a moment which is eternal, and thus, creation is eternal. From creation comes all awareness and all consciousness. As a result of becoming conscious, there emerges an understanding that one's beingness is contained within the oneness of all. This is what we refer to as the big bang, pop or bop, because all of you have popped or bopped along within your own moment of creation. What one chooses to do with that moment remains the choice of each individual.

As we move further into this explanation, it is important to realise that there is much which cannot be theorized accurately. If you contemplate an eternal moment of creation, a timeless point in which all things exist, do know that creation cannot stop and can never cease and so what has been, will always be. Science has adopted its own viewpoint on this, as have the various religions which provide their own spin on the subject. Alternatively, there are many who will challenge not only the perspectives of religion but those of science as well.

Most belief systems miss the object of what really should be contemplated - the very core of one's own inner self. It's the spirit contained within your body which should be the object of this pursuit. This is the true basis of creation. Therefore, from your physical situation, from that position, it is necessary to reverse the process and to reflect back within yourself. From there, you will have an opportunity to savour the real basis of creation. From the physical level where you exist at this time, if you look within, it will give you a truer appreciation of existence. Do realise that in the physical, you exist on an emotional level. It's most important for you to become cognizant of this fact, because the universal foundation for understanding is created upon an emotional basis.

Is there a conscious force, or what we call a God force, which is conscious of itself, and therefore, conscious of everything else simultaneously?

When you speak of a force, you refer to the force of That Which Is. It's difficult for some of you to grasp the concept of a totality. The idea of That Which Is includes you, it comprises us, and it encompasses everything. There remains no choice for such a force but to continue to create, due to the impetus of the continuous need to know through an on-going unfoldment. If that process ever stopped, then nothing would exist, and that's the difference between existence and non-existence.

Everything which is, is. You are. You are not only That Which Is, but also a part of everything which exists. Therefore, you exist. Your existence is realised through its own conscious feedback in relationship to yourself, and at the same time, to the physical universe.

Spirit must feel itself in the physical before it can realise its potential as spirit. Then it can reintegrate joyfully through a continuous interaction of spirit with the physical. The physical can only reside alongside of the existence of spirit, but on the contrary, spirit does not require the physical in order to be.

If spirit, however, is to acknowledge itself, it must recognise the physical as well. Both are inextricably tied into a wholeness and a oneness, whether on the personal level, which you know as your own individual physical self, or on a molecular or subatomic level which creates a piece of rock. For instance, a quartz crystal is a specific type of rock which is comprised of explicit types of atoms and molecules, held together in a particular way to create a particularized rock. It's the same with each individual.

Yes, but is there an ultimate consciousness or a supreme being, one which is conscious of the totality, a being that we would think of as God? I'm talking about a being which is simultaneously conscious of everything, and possessing an omniscience concerning all dimensions. Is this just a far out concept?

It's not a far out concept. This is what it all is! It cannot be separate from anything, and you are attempting to create division. In truth, self-awareness comes through an absolute understanding of existence validating itself through its very presence in all aspects of being, whether observable or not observable. That Which Is, is God, everything, there can be no more and no less.

How can you conceptualize that which is conceptualizing? If you can understand this thought, you will begin to understand and appreciate the wondrous components of which you are comprised. The elements which constitute you, are not just the physical you, but it's the questioning you, and the aware you, all of which must be considered. The awareness and comprehension that you hold, is but a reflection of the ultimate awareness and comprehension. When you feel within your own self, a correctness and a particular rightfulness concerning whatever you are doing, this is how you connect with the source. Then you know that you are following that which is your own decision in creation.

Some tend to think of God as pure love. Any comments?

When we speak of pure love, we speak of pure energetic love, just as you understand the feeling of love within you. This is the one connection which is universal. The energy which appears to be holding and binding all physical life together is, in fact, a physical representation of this sense of love. We have been attempting to provide you with an intellectual approach to God, and so the manner in which we have been presenting the God concept has been an attempt to meet that particular need.

Stepping away from this explanation, understand that God cannot be understood and contained within cut and dried concepts. What you refer to as God, is That Which Is. This includes you, it comprises us, and every molecule, atom, and all the space in-between. Everything in creation can be considered to be God. By directly connecting to this energy force, you can become conscious of it. We're not suggesting, however, that you could be unattached from it in the first place, for if you were, you would not exist.

So what is this place called heaven that people believe in?

You see here, each individual has his or her own concept of what came before, and what follows physical existence. In the larger sense, heaven can be envisioned as a place for the energies which are no longer in the physical form. Therefore, in this sense, you can speak of a heaven.

Wouldn't that be more of a state?

Yes, this would be more of a state, but however, you must understand that not everybody grasps this concept. It's important to include other descriptions of this state that many call heaven. For you see, a state is not something which can be tangibly measured, nor can it be perceptibly created. It's important to understand that a state is a concept, whereas heaven can be concretely envisioned as a place and this gives a balance and grounding to those who exist upon the physical plane. It is most important to understand that those who believe in a heaven will experience a heaven in their own particular way on passing from the physical.

Some people like to imagine their God concept as a person to whom they are praying. They envision a physical God, one who possesses feet, eyes, legs, and a human form. They are always talking to, or praying to a person. Please comment.

That Which Is, does not have a human form. It's but a reflection of your own creation to which you are speaking and connected. What you are reconnecting to, is that energy which is all of life, all of creation, and all of consciousness. Therefore, it is of great benefit to pray to this energy and to be appreciative, while at the same time, offering thanks for the creation of a state which allows the physical mind to become manifest and to be directed in a conscious way.

Previously, you had raised the question: Did humanity create God, or did God create humanity? As you are aware, humans tend to imagine God as a kind of omniscient, supernatural being, a totality which is conscious of everything going on, even knowledgeable about the activities of its own creations. Is there such a conscious being? Is what we term God or the universal consciousness, both separate from us and at the same time, a conscious unified entity in its own right.

These are conceptual misunderstandings, statements implying that universality must have a conscious state. This is not true, not in the manner in which you are questioning. God can only be described as a continuous expression of creation. The moment in which you are involved, all become involved in that moment as you pass through it. That is where consciousness exists.

Consider consciousness to be a brush fire moving swiftly through open fields of grass. The moment of the fire, the moment of the creation of this energy dispersal, occurs along one line, and one line only, leaving behind it a path which is not involved in the actual activity of burning.

Metaphorically speaking, it's the same manner in which you understand consciousness. There is each moment of your conscious existence and your direct connection to it. This is the only way in which it can be described in order for it to be understood on a third dimensional level. In truth, that is all there is, and yet, consciousness cannot become frozen or stuck in a conventional condition; it's always in a state of movement.

This is the very precept that ancient man began to appreciate, particularly regarding his mortality versus the apparent continuation of life after his demise. This concept was embellished over time, and subsequently, God became something separate from mankind. Currently, humanity continues to cling to this age-old belief: If humankind is contained within a larger picture, then as a result, this bigger picture must be smarter than humans, for it gets to exist forever.

Whereas in truth, the original understanding proclaimed that there was no separation, no division between conscious mind, humankind, animal life, rocks, and everything which exists - both hidden and visible. So you see, when humans began to define themselves apart from their world, a separation from that oneness emerged as a result of this differentiation, and thus, in one sense, placed humanity in the role of co-creators on its own planet.

Therefore, it is important to understand that there must first be a separation of consciousness from the mass consciousness, or That Which Is, to allow it to become an individualized creative aspect, thus holding a directive in its own right. This becomes your will, and will is what is directing everyone experiencing consciousness in the physical.

There is also the matter of evolution - the conscious evolution of consciousness in the physical. This allows spirit to become even more sophisticated, and to communicate more effectively not only with other physical beings, but also with other levels or planes within the conscious omniverse.

In this sense, and moving back to the God consciousness, in truth, the God consciousness is a collective consciousness comprising each and every aspect of creation, even to the smallest microbe, and to the minutest organism, molecule, electron and neutron. It doesn't matter for all are part of the one, and not just on a physical level but also connected by spirit throughout all of infinity - a pretty big place when one considers it.

Thus, it's a good idea to be appreciative of the consciousness which is being held within that earthly vessel that each of you is contained within - your physical body. By doing so, every person has an opportunity not only to experience one's separateness from the original source, but also, has the chance to rejoin that larger consciousness during the life experience on earth. So in fact, this consciousness, or God as humankind calls it, is not one which is self-directed, or aware in the sense that it be judgmental or that it has certain desires to direct mankind. Desires from mankind, in this sense, come from mankind's own concepts of what is necessary for a cooperative effort to continue growth and expansion as a sentient race.

Therefore, it's this original separation in thinking which leads to the question: Did man create God, or did God create man? In truth, this must be understood as the need of humanity to conceive of a God, and subsequently, to believe that humankind was created by it. At the same time, humankind must understand that its species is a part of this creative force, and therefore, not existing as isolated beings which are separate from it. In reality, by the very fact of their existence, humans are expressions of continuous creation.

Your description about the brush fire provided a very expansive viewpoint concerning how we project this entity we call God, and why we are praying to our own creations, which in one sense is still God.

In all senses, and we do not declare prayer to be silly or purposeless. By praying, one is actually reconnecting with the energy of That Which Is, as we had indicated in our metaphor regarding the brush fire. We can also use the metaphor of a wave. The structure of a wave as it moves through the ocean will alter, and yet, before the wave and after the wave the water is calm. It's the wave itself which creates and carries the energy.

This is much the same as how the life energy is carried. When an individual prays to this energy, that person is reconnecting with it and has the opportunity to have full access to everything contained within it. In other words, it's a matter of surrendering one's personal consciousness to the greater consciousness of continuous creation.

Therefore, it's not a matter of saying that there is no God in heaven, or that there is no point in praying. What is important to understand is that the energy which comes from praying is actually a physical manifestation of spirit's need to reconnect from time to time with its original source during the physical walk. It is much the same as when your car needs to receive gasoline every so many miles or it cannot continue. This is the manner in which prayer can serve as the highest format for each individual, especially for those who allow themselves to surrender to the greater energy.

Some will describe this as an ecstasy, others will recount it as an entity which appears to them and gives them something. Whatever is required by an individual to have this connection occur, when it does happen, then it is all the more convincing. There is no correct or incorrect way. It is only important that you bring this energy into your consciousness, so that each one of you has an appreciation of the validity of his or her own existence, and for the continuous, on-going process of creation.

Why do many people feel that they have been created directly by a God?

This is their Christian upbringing. This is the map or the overlay which was given during the formative years. What else can one believe? There is no other choice.

So there is no God existing in the form that most of us have been taught to believe?

Do you mean a big guy in the sky? There is only creative energy. We do not see this energy as a single, focussed mind which directs all activities in the universe. This concept is a creation of man and involves an idea of power and someone in charge. These are human characteristics which have been projected onto an entity which has even been deemed to have a bad temper. This depicts an angry God, a being who invokes fear and takes pleasure from it. It's a God who is there to coordinate the least little thing in everyone's life. If anyone thinks or does anything against this God, the result is punishment.

This is the understanding of many about what God is, but there is no God existing in the sense that the Christians believe. There is a creative energy we refer to as That Which Is. As far as this energy having a consciousness and sense of direction for everything within creation, there would be too much for this God to have on its plate to accomplish such a task. When you are in charge of infinity, it's very difficult to look after the atom in your left toe. There is no conscious directive from a greater being, although such ideas make people's lives simpler and give them a feeling that they are complete and have purpose. If someone is serving an eternal God, then they don't have to think about serving themselves or looking after their own growth and understanding. Their focus remains outside of themselves. Only self-awareness can take one beyond these beliefs.

This self-awareness comes through revelation. Revelation comes from understanding, and understanding comes through experience.

Unfortunately, there are many who continue to follow these archaic belief systems which contribute to a deterioration of the cultural fabric within which you exist. As long as these old belief systems continue to subsist within this fabric, then it will remain gabardine and never become virgin wool. Don't you just love our metaphors?

- 2 -

DEATH

Considering the death experience, let's take the situation when someone has just died and can no longer function within the physical body. Please take us forward from that point in the death process, and comment on what the awareness is, and what the guides do.

Each individual will go through an individualized death experience when crossing to the non-physical. It's important to understand that the beliefs held during the lifespan of each person will be projected beyond them. It's no different than what the mind does during physical existence, including the dream state. Following the ending of a physical life, the contents of one's consciousness continue to be projected outside of the self, and are further enacted in the form of a dream experience.

Death is a time of transition, and those things that an entity had believed to be truths during physical existence, will be represented and reflected into the after death experience. They are created by the mind, and the mind is totally responsible for creating one's experience.

You must understand what the mind truly is. Those who believe that the mind is just the brain miss out on certain facts. It's like saying that a radio in itself holds the power to broadcast. It's not true. The radio is a part of the process of the broadcasting power, which allows for the transmission. The radio receives information and subsequently, transmits it. This is what the brain does. The mind is that which contains what is inside of you. The mind is everything. It's that which perceives through the physical entity. In fact, the mind is the connecting tissue of the soul as well as the original energy of creation.

This is what the mind is. When we speak of a universal mind, we speak of the ultimate mind. It's the mind to which all belong. So there will never be a final answer to creation, because there will never exist a state of stasis. There are only states of movement and continual growth.

What happens following physical death is that the mind will create whatever is necessary to offer emotional protection to the deceased individual. Since the mind can no longer safeguard the individual physically, it will move in a direction to assist the entity emotionally. Such assistance includes reducing the amount of shock and trauma which follows the loss of a physical body. As well, the mind provides an understanding concerning the lack of connectivity to the body - the physical vehicle which emerged from the consciousness of the mind in the first place.

For some, there might have been shock or trauma on physical death. The crossing is a time when a unique world will be created for each departing consciousness as the transition period is entered. Guides will show themselves, and be represented in a form which is appropriate to the mental state of the entity which has just passed to the non-physical.

This enables the transition to be smooth and clear. If you consider the fact that on your planet alone, there are many thousands of deaths on a daily basis, be aware that all of them are being catered for in a similar manner. It's not set up as a factory, where those departing individuals show up in a waiting room and subsequently, remain there until the next thing happens. Due to the fact that mind and spirit are attended to in a manner that we have just described, each entity begins to look after itself by creating it's own view of the after world. Such representations are reproduced in a way which might seem rather odd or strange, but it's important for an individual to be comfortable and to feel safe after departing the physical existence.

Does the subconscious mind take over?

We prefer to call it the superconscious. It's not that it takes over, but it's as if that aspect of yourself, that failsafe mechanism which you had always sensed was there, automatically falls into place. When entities realize that they are in an altered state of consciousness, a state which is outside of the physical experience, some will be traumatized and freeze. If that happens, such entities will be visited by guides, or energies which represent the higher aspects of spirits which were known in life. Such beings will appear and offer comfort, as well as welcoming a departing personality back to a state of consciousness which is a part of the continuing and endless cycle of growth.

To understand this further, be aware that there is a change of attitude which accompanies the loss of a physical body. A sense of wonderment can emerge, it's a state that you have always held since childhood, but this condition becomes tainted and covered over during the life cycle. For many, death is a return to innocence, a view of the world from a new and pure understanding, a perspective which had long ceased to be for the conscious mind.

On passing, existence is revealed in its true magnificence. In this sense, the natural curiosity and reverence for That Which Is, including one's own being, is then processed. At that point, the true growth and development of the spirit emerges. This is a state whereby an entity realize that it must embrace not only its own self, but its own conscious state of wonder and wonderment. Also, it will feel and understand that through the recent death experience, it has truly emancipated itself from physical consciousness.

We don't mean that it will emancipate itself from the personality. Don't confuse consciousness with personality. Taking a simplistic view, personality can be considered to be the interaction of the spirit with the environment which surrounds it. Personality develops through a variety of different interactions, events, and numerous occurrences which have been experienced during physical life. It's a state of consciousness which is in a mode of continual modification. The personality of an individual, or that which you label as happy, sad, angry or whatever, understands itself to be in a constant process of change. After death, the personality experienced during life on the earth, will maintain its own individuality and consciousness, but it will transform itself in its ability to understand and appreciate itself through itself.

If an individual plans to ask for one's guides, or for their assistance - would such help be instantaneous and forthcoming? Is this the best form of preparation?

Yes, in that sense, of course. It's a part of the preparatory aspects of physical existence. Such activity helps to incorporate the advantages of physical life into the non-corporeal state of being.

When one releases the physical reference points at death, plus all of one's linkage to the earth and to a physical body, you are saying that the connections to one's spiritual state happen automatically, and it's not something that we can really envision very well from our current human point of view.

Yes.

What we call an earthbound spirit, or an earth personality which has crossed and clings desperately to its physical reference points, such as in a haunting - what causes this situation?

Partly, it's a belief system, particularly if there was a physical addiction to drugs, sex, liquor, tobacco, and the list goes on and on. These are all physical cravings.

In our calculation of time, how many years might an entity cling to physical existence after death? Can it go on for hundreds of years?

Forever. They have the same rights and the same energies as all entities do, energies reflecting the light and the energy of That Which Is, which is eternal as you would understand it. Therefore, it will be forever, or until they decide to change their minds.

Those departing entities, the ones who are sexually addicted and so on - do they hang around brothels, pubs, and similar environments? As a spirit - do they focus on those places in the physical?

They simply roam the world, considering within themselves the need to express their addictions. They invade the consciousness of individuals who have neither the strength nor the energy to release them. Also, they are attracted to physical beings whose auras will respond to them in this way. As well, they are drawn to those who are within intense emotional situations, often teenagers who are undergoing puberty. This is a time when there are many changes occurring within the body, and with the physiological alterations occurring, it attracts these particular types of energies.

Even though some people talk about possession or entities who come to invade in this manner, they cannot possess. What is really controlling these individuals who think they are possessed, is their own beliefs, but as you are aware, beliefs are what make the world real. Individuals, who are supposedly under attack or possession, are afraid of the outpouring of their own imaginations, as if they will be incapable of changing things.

Those who crossover, need to let go of things of the physical, including addictions. Their process is not necessarily to hang around areas which held their addictions, but they do continue to hold connections to their addictions. At death, what they experience within themselves, is a projection of the addictive behaviour. At times, their energies will be felt in certain areas, particularly places which they had frequented while physically embodied. They are not necessarily out on the streets looking for spots to hang out. This would be counter indicative to their condition. As these entities cross, they are devoid of an understanding of their total situation, and therefore, they require a certain degree of healing.

Being physically embodied, many of us have addictions, even though some are rather simple such as caffeine. Can you define addiction for us?

Addiction means that you cannot physically live without something. There are things which bind a person to the life process and not always to the upside. There are many addictions, and an addiction is something that you cannot live without. It is not only that you need it, but that you have to have it. It can be drugs, gambling, alcohol, food, sex, anything which touches the senses can become a danger. Addiction occurs when you lose control and move beyond what is considered to be normal propriety. When you are pushing people out of the way to get to the buffet, or fighting somebody over the last peace of cheesecake, you have a problem with food. Addictions are previous experiences which have gotten out of hand. They become obsessions in particular ways.

So if these earthbound energies are so heavily addicted, then they can stay in that state forever. Can they just pass from one generation to another? An example would be someone who lived in the 1600's and was addicted to alcohol - could that spirit still be active today?

Yes, but often in one of its favourite hangouts. Be aware that this is too simplistic an explanation of how this works. Do not misinterpret this information and declare it as exactly what happens. In fact, it is only our way to describe what occurs, not actually what transpires. For outside of the physical, there is no time. When these entities enter into the non-physical, they exist in a real world surrounded by their own understanding. Part of that world is an interconnection with the physical world which intersects at certain key locations which you refer to as vortexes. These vortexes or movements of energy can be quite powerful and timeless because there is no concept of time outside of your dimension. There are only hundreds of years in your linear way of viewing time. When we say forever, it also means instantly; for where there is no time, both are one and the same.

So it's like an eternal moment, that's where they are, non-specific, until awareness kicks in.

Yes, and regarding circumstances that people attribute to the activity of ghosts, many occurrences are based upon certain psychic impressions which occur during moments of high emotional discharges by someone holding physical sentience. Certain energies are discharged directly into the physical environment, much the same way in which energy is contained within an orgone box. So particular human energies, or negative energies or even spirits, can often leave energy trails, and thus bequeath an emotional discharge which remains stuck in a certain area long after an individual has left the physical plane and no longer has any need to remain in that zone from a spiritual aspect.

Regarding the events of September 11th, 2001, after the exploding of the World Trade Centre - what happened spirit side with the sudden crossing of all of those people after their traumatic experiences?

Speaking from the moment that the deaths occurred, the deaths came in three waves, as you witnessed it. The first wave was the crashing, the explosions were the second, and the third was the collapsing of the buildings. As these entities crossed over, as occurs in all cases of this nature, they were mercifully taken by instantaneous death. One moment an entity was physically alive, and the next it was not. The consciousness being in a condition of shock or trauma after the event underwent a situation of helplessness, or something close to what you would know as the delta state of relaxation. It was from this state that these entities were taken, not to a particular place as you would understand it, but in a mind sense, to a situation of recuperation and reorientation regarding their condition. This is what occurred on what you call the metaphysical side.

What happened to the perpetrators of that event, the hijackers who believed that they were going to heaven by committing such acts in the name of Allah?

The same process occurred for those beings as well, but they entered into a double recuperation because of the shock of finding out that the other side is not as they had anticipated. Transition is difficult for those who are perpetrators of great shifts. Although part of their purpose was to create the shift, the method of their deaths was of their own choosing. You would refer to their actions as an altering of the fabric of life.

Afterwards, were they lucid, and did they realise what they had done?

Yes, in one sense, but they were beyond caring. In truth, what they did holds a different significance in the spiritual levels.

Would the entities who committed those acts have reunited with their higher selves?

Yes, as you understand it, that took place. They entered into a state of reunification and a situation of being nurtured and understood. For you see, in this placeless place and timeless time, spirit is beyond good and evil. Usage regarding these terms is strictly relative to belief systems which are held in third dimensional existence. It is important for you to understand the intricacies of this changeover from the physical into spirit.

If the perpetrators of those deeds have realized their actions - are they truly beyond good and evil?

Yes, you must be aware that what has been played out is a balancing of the energies on the earth plane. Up to that time, mankind had been progressing, but now that progress is accelerating at a faster rate and expanding exponentially. The point that humankind has reached in its understanding of science and technology, invites elements which will challenge such developments. It causes a counterforce, which is always there to ensure that there is a failsafe regarding the growth of any physical organism or organisation.

What is occurring at present is a part of the natural order of things. It's important to realise that there are factions at work which are struggling for the consciousness of the world. This is where the world is standing at this time. It's a battle of wills, a fight between technology and fundamental religious beliefs. Such religious convictions are self-defeating by the very causes that they uphold. Religion can only remain alive as long as it is injected with change.

You stated that those who crossed on September 11th, 2001, due to the events of the World Trade Centre in New York, entered into a delta state or a situation of rest and recuperation. Were they catered for by their guides and others?

Yes, and in fact, the most flexible of those energies passed quickly beyond this state. It's was a cognitive acceptance of their altered reality, which allowed for a transition of their complete consciousness at that point.

For those on the aeroplanes - would that have been their chosen time for crossing?

Do understand that the chosen time for crossing, is somewhat of a fallacy in the way that you understand it. It was really a moment of juncture for these entities to transition into spirit. Outside of the time dimension, there is a timelessness in which these entities had already existed and not existed, particularly in regard to the corporeal forms that they held during their physical lives. Therefore, the transition was instantaneous, and this ties into being able to understand how the energy of an individual remains in an eternal state.

Hypothetically, if I were to cross right now - what would I experience?

If you are asking for the process, it is difficult for us to indicate what would happen for you in particular. As you understand from our previous conversations, each individual creates a personalized after death state on passing. This is an oxymoron in itself, for in reality, it's a state of rebirth. In moving into the non-physical dimension, at the outset there is a transmutation of energy.

In order to maintain the next step on the journey and to be conscious while moving into that next state, there is a gathering together of the identity of an individual. It's more like a concentration into the self. The most complete transition is one you have planned. The better you prepare, the greater the opportunity for particular outcomes to occur as you translate from the third dimension into that of spirit.

Regarding the death process, and when we begin to cross over, we still have our physical reference points, we still hold to this physical identity. You have mentioned that all of a sudden, when we become non-physical, a different awareness kicks in, perhaps more of a connection with the superconscious. It's a realization that we're so much more, not only a composite of all the other personalities that our soul has led or is leading, but our awareness becomes enhanced. You have stated that after physical death, the reality of the soul becomes self-explanatory in itself. This awareness transcends our trying to conceptualize it here on earth, and it becomes a case of - so that's it! Physical death conforms to a situation whereby one understands automatically. Is this truly what will happen for those who can accept that they are no longer physical?

Yes.

If one is clinging to physical existence - does it just take more time?

You may put it this way as well, however, this is a moot point in relationship to what we are speaking about here.

When people speak about astral planes, causal planes, and so forth - is this terminology to be understood only within the physical reference points?

No, these are states which truly exist along with physical existence. Reference materials such as the Egyptian Book of the Dead, as it has been translated, and also the Tibetan Book of the Dead, which has also been translated, are recommended. The best editions are those by W. Evans Wentz.

You will understand that through the study of these texts, there are varying degrees of change that one goes through on leaving the body. For a short while during the transition, it's important for the departing consciousness to be connected with those who have cared for it at some point. This allows that energy to pass, and also for it to connect to other levels of consciousness as they are raised over a period of approximately three weeks, speaking in terms of your measurement of time.

Every passing is, however, individualized. It is created by each departing personality's need to experience a release from the physical. Do understand that all those in the physical are programmed to the core of their entire being to maintain life. Life does not let go of the physical easily, that is, the life which is instilled within the physical existence.

Do not mistake the spirit for physical intellect which is a by-product of the physical. When we speak of spirituality, there is no bigger or smaller spirit within one entity or another. All are equally valid. Therefore, on the spirit level, you are dealing with a different degree of consciousness, one which does not invalidate the physical, but it is something which is separate and apart from it, and yet, a part of it during the physical experience. Following the cessation of the physical form, the spirit has an opportunity to step outside of the body, and simply, to change its perspective while reflecting on the next level of consciousness that it holds.

On passing from physicality into spirit, you can observe the denseness of the physical, and there are various levels of density or what you might think of as grossness. So what you refer to as the astral plane is what could be considered to be the next level. It is just outside of the physical but also within it. Therefore, in a sense, it maintains weight on the spiritual level. Once raised above that level, it's the same as if you are departing the atmosphere of the earth.

An example in your terms of reference, would be moving from the atmosphere into the stratosphere and then into the emptiness of space. In the emptiness of spirit, you would understand the true emptiness which must exist in the first place for spirit to enter into self-cognition. Without that vacuity, there could be no motivation to maintain conscious will or to desire growth.

What awaits those on the other side who have committed suicide?

First, they have to re-establish their truth. What a suicide is really about, is relinquishing the value of one's life and abandoning the gift of physical animation and physical exchange. A suicide's life has become so devalued and worthless, that he or she no longer holds any value or worth in existence. When these individuals pass over, immediately, other entities will rush to catch them as they arrive. By whatever means necessary, there is an attempt to help them to understand and to re-establish the basis of their own spirituality. Suicides will be disorientated. The souls who assist are there to allow these spirits once again to balance their energies and to come into equilibrium.

Do you have anything to say to any reader who might be contemplating such an act because of his or her life's situation?

Each individual must make a personal decision based on one's own life. The only thing that we can say in regards to life and death is that the life that you have chosen to live, is the life that you opted for in order to be on the earth. Initially, it was your choice. If you choose to leave early through your own undertaking, that's your option. Be aware though, that the truth which comes from learning is not derived through leaving but in staying. The basis for growth is founded upon the lessons that you learn. In particular, one of the lessons is learning to focus on the value of your own life, and not on its worthlessness based upon what society or others deem to be of value.

For example, those who leave because of bankruptcy, had driven themselves to a situation of making as much money as possible because they feared being bankrupt. What they wound up with was their greatest fear. All human beings will experience their greatest fears during their lifetime, whether it is poverty, bankruptcy, desertion, loneliness or death. Your fears will come upon you because you have concentrated on them. It's important to understand that it's a person's focus which brings an individual to a particular point of experience. In reality, individuals such as the bankrupts had been focussing on their fears although they might have thought otherwise. It's a result of continually attempting to move away from whatever it is that you fear. People bring these things into their lives because they spend more time considering what they don't want, rather than what they do want.

Your phrase regarding the necessity of changing our perspective of existence, this is what I think we miss out on here because we try to transfer our current human perspectives of reality into the after world. With this change of perspective that you speak about - are you saying that it happens automatically if one is open to it?

Yes, and one will be aware of the possibility and practicality of this occurring. Those who enter into the passing with clear and open minds and with hearts which are excited about discovering the next phase of being are the ones who will have the greatest degree of clearness in their passing. The ones, who hold onto fundamentalist fear beliefs, are the departing personalities who will experience the most difficult crossing, and in fact, are the same ones who will report experiences of hell following their near death episodes.

Yes, because the mind creates those conditions. Would that be the same as an experience right after death, when one clings to physical references and feels the sensation of a physical body, but it's just the mind creating that feeling because that's what the entity is used to experiencing?

For the first couple of days, it is necessary for the departing entity to understand that the physical body is no longer functioning. This must be realized, and subsequently, any connection to it needs to be released. It's as if you were looking at your hair which has just been cut and lays motionless on the floor of the barber shop. Unless you have a strong desire to pick it up and then stick it back on your head because you are going to take it with you, it will be left behind and you will continue on in your journey. It's much the same in understanding what we have just described.

So, on first crossing, an individual maintains the psychological and emotional identity that one had as a human personality. Does the rigidity of this personality and psychological structure begin to dissipate as the higher aspects of one's being begin to filter through?

Ah ha, now you know what will happen when you personally will cross over.

So each new personality or physical lifetime, is the creation of the soul, which on passing or physical death, still maintains that psychology but also much more.

Yes, this occurs when the departing personality interconnects with that which it has been extrapolated through, and emerged from.

After death, if a departing personality clings to physicality - does such an entity experience a more difficult process?

Yes and what you must understand is this: That Which Is, is available on all levels, and it does not necessarily require a physical form in order to be. One of the difficulties that all of you experience on the plane where you exist currently, is that you believe something cannot be alive without some physical representation. It's an interesting but particularly one-sided view.

These explanations always seem to be so far beyond our ways of thinking and how we experience things. Is it possible that we can only arrive at glimpses of it? I'm talking about understanding infinite concepts.

The truths of existence are great simplicities. They are not complicated or convoluted. Each consciousness takes these mysteries into account in its attempt to understand its place in the physical. Does it make sense or seem logical that an entity would be created to have consciousness and awareness, only to have it extinguished at some point during its existence? Therefore, most forget to include their pre-existence prior to physical life. It's important to understand the process. The fear of not being on earth is what prevents many from having a successful transition. There are those who do have extreme difficulty and in fact, become trapped on the physical levels.

I'm beginning to understand that the more rigidly we hold to our concepts of a physical ego and earthly existence, that the less able we are to experience these other states. Is this accurate?

Yes, that's the basis of it. Any practitioner of Buddhism will tell you that what you are saying is true. It's important to let go, and then to allow the process of existence to flow through you without any discrimination on your part, or any attempt to alter this flow through your conscious direction.

What about those who are unable to let go of their preconceptions regarding the afterlife?

You must understand the nature of reality. It is different for each individual as they perceive it. We shall take a moment here, to allow you to appreciate the miracle of your own ability to create. Your creation on the plane where you presently exist might include the birth of your children, along with the life that you have developed. This is your ability to interact on the physical plane.

Outside of the physical plane, you also interact by creating your own reality on that level. Therefore, it is your perception, and only your perception which counts. It is not that you imagine what is happening in the non-physical, but on that level, you actually experience it. For that is the totality of any experience. It's being in the moment and experiencing it, without giving consideration to anything else outside of it. This is the ability you have here as well, but some have difficulty enacting this while on earth.

You see, many of you are insistent upon discovering another place, so getting to heaven becomes similar to going somewhere in a car. This is not how it works. If that were possible, then there would be no need for considering the physical as an alternative aspect of being. The truth is, that both the physical and the non-physical are contained within the same aspect of existence. The only difference is the side of the fence that you are sitting on at any given time. Your conceptualizations of the other side preclude your experience. Your conceptualization of the after death state cannot be equal to what is contained there. This is what creates the difficulty for many of you.

Some people imagine floating around in thin air.

We have not said that it's a case of floating around in space. This is how some individuals conceive things which do not fit or conform to their current reality.

How can they move beyond those imaginings?

The spirit world is not an empty space. In fact, the spirit world is a place full of energy, interconnections, communication, love, harmony, and continuous and on-going creation. For it is from the spirit world that the physical world originates. Therefore, it's important for you to understand that our world as it is, is not a place, it's a state.

It is difficult to explain what a state is using your terminology. You might understand it in this way: You are in a physical state of existence, and within your physical state, there are certain rules and regulations which bind you to the physical, such as the physical laws contained within your current reality. For you to exist on your plane, these must be adhered to. When there is a passing of life from your plane the rules change. In fact, the whole aspect changes to the greater whole.

It is difficult to explain things outside of this, other than to say, that the physical experience is contained within the spiritual understanding, and indeed, this is the true situation. It's as if one returns to the spirit plane, and into an area which you would refer to as heaven in your understanding. What is important, however, is the energetic connection to the place. We are using the word place to indicate an altered state which is not of your dimension. So do understand that it is not specifically a space in the middle of nothing. There are countless billions of energetic entities within the non-physical existing in a condition that you would naturally interpret as a heavenly state of being, but it's nothing like the third dimension.

Have you any words for people who have a great concern about being able to communicate with their deceased relatives?

This is a needless worry. In fact, they are surrounded by their love, and indeed, they will have the ability to reconnect. It is important to let go of the concept of not having it happen. Instead, it's necessary to focus upon where one is going, rather than where one has been.

To understand the after death state, you must think outside of the third dimension. In a situation of non-physicality, you do not have to worry about the concepts of others, or dimensions, or any other aspect, all you have to do is simply move into the flow of what is occurring.

We understand that there are many who are in pain in your world, surrounded by the grief of physical events. Many are attempting to ask for a universal concept regarding a place called heaven, due to the conceptualization of a heaven which originated during childhood. This creates great difficulty and misunderstanding, resulting in misinterpretations of what happens after physical death. Many beliefs have been taught by the church, and therefore, must be seen for what they truly are - a controlling device created to maintain order on the physical plane. This is so the church can take hold of individuals and thus control their earthly journeys.

In truth, this is a misrepresentation of that which came down in an oral tradition from the Master. No one was recording Jesus' words when he existed on earth; there were only those who were recounting his stories. Therefore, much of what the Master said, was lost in the translation of these stories, particularly events such as your biblical references to his Father's kingdom. This creates a concept which becomes very confusing especially in your time, because the ancient idea of a kingdom is no longer understood in modern terms.

In times gone by, the word kingdom was very specific and referred to the degree of energy a ruler would have within a specified area, and to the amount of control that a person in power would hold regarding a specific realm. Humanity has now progressed beyond the need to be controlled by kingdoms, and in fact, has evolved beyond creating kingdoms at all. So instead, that whole idea was turned into the creation of a heaven.

In truth, non-physical existence allows a soul to regenerate and recreate, and in many instances, to participate in physical conditions through a conscious connection with those who were known in life, as well as with those whom one has never met but is connected to through soul.

So this is what's important in these situations. It's not to have a brilliant vision concerning the afterlife, but to possess more of a feeling concept. This is what is needed, a kinaesthetic appreciation of what is going on. For some of you, words are simply rhetoric and only physical touch is reality. This is what must be appreciated, particularly in those who are suffering a great loss or have experienced enormous grief.

Would the souls from medieval times, those who continued to desire physicality, still be acting out their scenarios from hundreds of years ago, because the astral is a timeless zone? Would there be communities of them?

No, not as you are imagining it, not in that way. All who arrive in spirit will eventually find their way through. What you are describing would be known as a haunting on the physical plane. That's a matter of different energies.

What about people who associate pain with the afterlife, such as those who believe in hell and eternal suffering?

When they pass over, they will not be sent to hell. They'll go somewhere much nicer. They will go to what humans think of as heaven, where they will experience a classic reconstruction of their lives on earth. They'll see the good parts and observe the bad. They will look at the portions in which they caused pain in others, and then see the pain which others caused in them. Most important, they will be shown how they grew from the elementary beliefs held at the beginning of their lives, to a convergent view of the world at the end.

People, who have led a relatively sombre and innocent life, will not undergo those hellion types of experience that some believe take place. Again, we emphasize that you will experience your own visions of what you believe an afterlife would be like. Such imaginings create a degree of familiarity, allowing individuals to achieve a greater totality of understanding as they gather together their physical experience.

There is no physical type of hell after death. There is only the hell which can occur during physical life. Hell is a metaphor for a state of discomfort, regret, guilt, penance or retribution. Traditionally, it has been conceived of as a place where one is paid back by the universe for transgressions in physical life. This is a vision propagated by Christianity to force its members to toe the line. There have been common concepts of hell as being a place which is somewhat hot and comprised of pools of lava, but an Eskimo might picture hell as eternal winter, a vision of frozen torment rather than a heated one.

The burning version owes its existence to those who inhabited the more temperate climates. Rather than worrying about ending up in such a place, we suggest that you concern yourselves more with those who have been feeding you these lies. Hell is not a place; it's a belief concocted by those bent on exerting control and holding others through fear.

Heaven has been envisioned as the opposite of paying for one's deeds in life. The classically portrayed heaven in Christian terms is known in other beliefs as the blue road of the afterlife, the happy hunting ground, the seat of heaven, the rivers of Babylon, and so on. There are terms in all religions which refer to retribution for deeds committed in the physical. There is no heaven and there is no hell, either above the earth or inside of it. Those who believe in hell while watching a volcano erupt, might imagine that this type of fate awaits all sinners. The opposite vision holds true for someone gazing at a blue sky imbued with a rainbow, or a person enjoying the colours of a beautiful sunset while listening to birds sing amidst the scent of beautiful flowers. Would this not be heaven?

These third dimensional physical concepts are the only reference points that most people possess. They are created by the earth experience. As everyone has felt ecstasy and agony, people transfer the same experiences to the non-physical. Therefore, in spiritual terms, ecstasy is assigned to heaven and anguish and agony to hell. All of it has been transferred from human experience. This is not the way things truly are.

Those who believe in heaven and hell as realities beyond the physical will only be trapped in this vision. By gauging their actions in life, they take on the worries and concerns created by their particular beliefs concerning an afterlife. All those who come onto your plane are highly moral beings prior to their arrival. This is the spirituality contained within all human beings. The extent to which this spirituality is directed during one's lifetime, and how growth takes place in one direction or another, depends on one's experiences.

On passing, those who firmly believe in a heaven and a hell might experience being tried, and then being released into heaven. The ultimate outcome, however, is that they will not go to a hell place. Even though on passing, an understanding might arise in these individuals that punishment is an option for them, it will be a result of their own belief systems. Sometimes, during the earth lives of individuals who hold beliefs in heaven or hell, a point is reached where such people truly believe within themselves that there has been a resolution, and that there has been forgiveness. This is part of the human psyche which prepares each individual for the passing.

All of this is so difficult for humans to understand. Will this become clearer when we cross?

People do not need to wait until they cross to understand what we are saying. We wish to reassure you of this outcome. The direction, in which your interests take you, can provide you with answers to any nagging little questions. Those answers will provide satisfaction, and allow individuals to carry on with their own process by assisting them to rise above such worries and doubts within this lifetime. This is part of each individual's on-going development, allowing things to be understood experientially and not just intellectually. You have to experience and feel things for them to be real for you. Experiential means having an inner certainty concerning things which cannot always be proven to others in an empirical way.

When crossing over, if the personality doesn't die or dissipate, will the soul continue to possess this current personality which has become a part of it? Isn't the present earth personality a part of a composite with all of the other personalities that a soul has lived?

It's the same way as you progress through your life. You had your time in childhood, a stage when you dealt with the world in that way, but you are no longer that person, and yet, that person lives within you. You are no longer the self-negating teenager with those feelings of insecurity, but just because those feelings have dissipated from that period in your life, some parts of you remain as that person. You should not think of the personality as static; it's always in a continual state of becoming and being, and therefore, you cannot say whom or what is important to you, until you achieve or reach particular periods in your life.

When a very young child dies - what happens to that personality? Is it cared for by souls on the other side which will appear in the form of its grandparents or whatever?

As you understand, all souls are eternal. In other words, the soul is not defined by the personality. The personality is defined by the soul. When a child passes from the physical into spirit, it returns to its original understanding and to its eternal process. We are using words to help you to understand this within your own parameters. As a result, it is not as if there is a cosmic nursery awaiting children on the other side.

To those who have lost a child, we want you to know that the process of crossing is very easy as that young person enters into the spirit state. Also, know that the personality of a child, just as the personality of any individual, becomes part of the total process of that soul's journey. The child's personality will expand and become part of its original energy. This is what occurs.

It's the same as if we were to speak of one's concept of God in tangible terms. There is no one correct way, for each of you creates your own individual path, whether within the physical or out of it. So to a large extent, the same process occurs for a child as it does for an adult. Often, the transition is much easier in the case of children, because there is not a lot of questioning or fear involved.

So those energies are incorporated back into the soul, and once again, an understanding and awareness automatically takes place, just as it does for any adult.

Yes, and for example, recall a time when you were a child. You did not feel childish in your mind, nor did you feel out of place in relationship as to who you were in the world at that time. The state of awareness and consciousness remains consistent and constant, no matter at what point in life the crossing takes place.

When we are physically awake and conscious on the earth plane - is our higher self conscious in another form within another dimension such as yours, while at the same time, conscious in the physical experience?

Yes, to a degree, as you have put it in this way. It is important, however, not to become enamoured concerning one's higher self. The aspect of a higher self should not be given too much emphasis. The conscious mind is the basis for decisions in any one lifetime.

Time is a human concept which we've created from our own perceptions based on how we experience reality here. What we physically experience here in the third dimension, is what most people imagine the non-physical to be like. Willows, if I'm not mistaken, that's the error that the majority of us make when we project our experience of reality from the third dimension into other dimensions, because we can't even conceive of them.

Correct, it is impossible not to do this, and in fact, impossible for any mind in the third dimension not to conceive in this way. Therefore, non-physical concepts would appear to be disjointed and seem to make no sense, if they were brought into the consciousness of the third dimensional mind as it is structured. So such concepts can only be understood outside of the physical, in other words, in the spirit state.

If someone wishes to enter into what is referred to as the Akashik or Hall of Records, the necessary state required to accomplish this occurs outside of the third dimension. Indeed, it's not a place that one goes to, but a place that one is, as well as corresponds to, at all times. Therefore, rather than going to, one is there. Again, it's difficult to conceptualize, until one is in that state, and suddenly, one is there. Arrival at this Hall of Records occurs outside of the third dimension, but it's not a place that you go to, it is a place that you are. This is not a concept but an actual fact. It's a state which exists outside of space, and again, difficult to understand because such information is contained within. Therefore, it is not your imagination, but in fact, it's your attendance which is required.

This is how things operate in other dimensions - using your terminology of dimensions for convenience sake - and it is important to see how this works. So it's the same in all aspects when it comes to how you create your concepts regarding existence outside of the third dimension, while simultaneously, you appear to be contained within it.

When someone dies, is that entity in an astral body? Is the astral body just another form which is dropped as the consciousness moves into a higher awareness?

You must not think of it as a vehicle that you can hop into, meld with, and then fly away. The truth is that the astral body contained the spirit before the physical, and it will do so after the physical. The astral body is a form of spirit, and therefore, it's not something that one would wear, but rather it is something which one is.

Yet, humans talk in terms of astral projection and an astral body. Do you say that an astral body or a mind body, are just physical terms of reference?

Understand that in a sense both are represented in the aura - an energy pattern existing inside and outside of the physical body which can be observed. It's this energy which is often referred to as the astral body, which permeates the physical body and is connected to the physical plane. In this sense, all individuals have their own gravitational field surrounding them. Yet, it is not gravity as you would understand it through classical physics. It is a physical representation of the true energy which is contained within the body, as the spirit is always larger than the physical vehicle, being both inside and outside of the body at all times.

The reason for this energy field is that it is important to have senses outside of the physical which are alive and well. This energy field allows physical beings to continue to remain intuitive to the spiritual connections from which they had originated, and also, to continue to maintain a connection to the physical body from within. As well, it is important to see that this auric pattern is necessary for the effective functioning of the body, specifically, the autonomic systems as well as the thinking processes, and of course, the comprehensive aspects of being consciously aware of your own being.

We say conscious awareness, for it is important to understand, that the life energy is expressed through individual souls coming onto your plane, and yet, all are part of the same oneness. Therefore, from a Judeo-Christian viewpoint, all are a part of creation. Keeping this in mind - as we give you an energetic understanding of how the aura is contained about the body - its senses are there to connect you with the environment and to bring your intuitions into a greater balance.

So when we use terms such as astral body, mind body and so on - are people simply referring to different levels of energy?

The reference should be to different vibrational states rather than levels of energy. If you are wondering about how to experience them, it can be done through the development of a quiet mind. The quiet mind becomes the fertile playground for new visions and new activities.

Do people really have an astral body, or is it something which is created by the mind when consciousness enters into another dimension or plane?

All entities have an astral body. It's contained within your dimension and outside of it at the same time. This not only creates, but manifests one of the basic tenets of existence - the ability to be in two places simultaneously. Most human beings have no understanding that this is an ability that they have, but every time they think, they are not only on the physical plane but on a different one as well.

Regarding astral projection, the spirit body exists independent of the physical body, and in fact, not only existed prior to the creation of the physical body but will exist after its dissolution. If you wish to call this spirit body the astral body, it's as good as any other description you might use to portray basic spirit energy.

How does the astral body vary from the etheric body and the mental body?

The etheric is aligned with the physical body and allows it to exist. The astral body can be seen more as an aura, with the aura being the representation and a reflection of the astral body. The aura has two levels, that is, there is a spiritual aura and a physical aura. The physical aura is a reading of the manifestation of the body and the life energy within it. The non-physical aura which exists in-sync with the physical aura is the spirit or astral body. This is the aspect which has the ability to move about, far beyond the physical body. There are many books which have been written on the subject of astral projection. Much information is available at this time.

How does the astral body differ from the mental body or the causal body?

The astral and the mental bodies are of the mind. Everything is contained within the mind. The mind is all. It's not separate from, but it is the mind which contains That Which Is. If the mind did not consciously grasp what went on around it at one level or another, or if there were no consciousness to observe something, then nothing would exist. The mind does not stand outside of causality. It's important to note that the astral body, the physical body, and everything that you can perceive, falls within the parameters of the mind. So do not separate things in this way. Everything operates together. There is no advantage in separating them. By doing so, you move away from understanding personal growth and become more interested in studying and isolating specific aspects of creation.

So it's better not to dissect or to separate such things as the soul and the mind body. Are you saying that it is all one consciousness?

After awhile, it becomes an intellectual exercise. For those who wish to be philosophical and to carry on great discussions about the fundamental facts of life, then dissecting and separating is ideal for their purposes. For others who don't want to fool around with the obvious and are serious about getting in touch with the true essence of their being, these are the people to whom we are presenting this information.

Why do individuals have different coloured auras?

It has to do with each person and the individuality of each being. As many have said, all souls were created at the same time, and we would not disagree with this statement. Each soul is unique in its own energy pattern. The colour of the aura is representative of an energy pattern. It's much the same as humanity records fingerprints. The aura operates as a fingerprint for the energy activating a physical body.

Do these fingerprints or energy patterns change during a person's lifetime, depending on one's interests, lifestyle and activities?

Generally not, although from time to time the aura might change colour due to certain feelings, emotions or health issues.

Individuals might be able to accept what you say emotionally, but often the difficulty we have is grasping it at the conceptual level. Although we might sense the truth of what you reveal emotionally - how can it be better understood on a conceptual basis?

What you are seeking here, is for us to give you an answer to the unanswerable. You are looking for a solution to the unsolvable. It's an attempt to obtain knowledge of the unknowable. Everything that we have been presenting to you in word form can only point to the actual truth of what is being conveyed. There can never be a manual on the tenets of reality. There can only be a philosophy surrounding it.

As we have indicated, people have their own individual vision and viewpoints about the truth. The ultimate answers and the information that one might be seeking, do not constitute the basis of reality, but in fact, are only questions about existence. Existence is, and that's the truth. Existence cannot be denied, any more than you can deny your own consciousness or your awareness of that which takes place all around you. As well, you cannot repudiate the consciousness of those about you who hold within themselves their own life force.

The ultimate truth boils down to one simple thing: When you look at another, what you are seeing is a reflection of your own self. Within each individual exists the truth of life, the truth of spirit, and the truth of being. So you don't have to sit around and continually worry about this, that, or any other thing which might enter your consciousness to mess things up. You don't have to be concerned about how others affect you in one way or another. Once you have reached a certain state of consciousness, your understanding of things becomes very simplistic, in much the same manner as we have explained it to you. It's one thing, however, to understand something cognitively, but quite another to experience it.

- 3 -

SOUL

When referring to non-physical beingness, there are numerous beliefs that alternative realities exist beyond the human level. These are states of consciousness that we can never appreciate fully, or be capable of knowing from our limited third dimensional perspective. Can you take us from our outlook as humans, and provide us with an understanding of consciousness within the non-physical to gain some insight into what constitutes a greater consciousness.

When you start to speculate about your spiritual state, first of all, you must begin with the understanding that there is only one mind shared by all participants within creation. Within that whole, there is the gift of differentiation. That distinction allows the one consciousness to perceive itself as separate from itself through different facets of its being. Although this might sound confusing, to truly understand it, we'll use the example of a glass of water.

If you toss water into the air, you will observe that it beads and breaks up. Each element as it separates remains the same as the water which stayed in the glass. When the various segments hit the ground, each will follow its own path. Some might sink into the earth while others will land on the surrounding terrain. The drops which might fall onto various flowers still retain their original molecular structure even though a separation from the whole had occurred.

This analogy is similar to the creation of separate beings from the universal consciousness. Thus, each individual not only contains that consciousness within, but also has the opportunity to realize a connection to the whole, while at the same time, observing the beauty of one's own unique separateness. This is perhaps the easiest way to describe your connection to the oneness. Often, the simplicity of the truths of existence becomes lost within the complexity of attempting to comprehend only the mysteries of the physical organism.

Humanity has survived within the earth's environment due to the evolution of mankind as a physical being. As a life form, humankind has developed the ability to be a true creator and co-creator on the physical level. Within each individual, there exists an understanding of not only the opportunity to create on the physical level, but also the occasion to reconnect with the original creative source. Simply put, this is the purpose of life as you would see it.

The mere mention of God brings up all sorts of images in people's minds, as we are conditioned to conceptualize in a certain way. This occurs also when people attempt to comprehend the soul.

As to the soul, any wording and classifications that we provide are not to be carved in stone. Our descriptions act only as touch points. What is soul? It's the relationship between a consciousness and that which gave it the consciousness. That is soul. To determine the semantics of using oversoul versus soul, or employing other descriptors such as conscious, unconscious, superconscious, and all of the other references to consciousness, the best way to conceptualize this, is to use another non-specific term, such as the way it is presented in Mahayana Buddhism where all is referred to as Mind. This is the same approach taken in Zen.

In that Mind, the consciousness of each individual becomes part of That Which Is. Therefore, you might say that this consciousness evolves and then erupts in a physical sense. This consciousness, this Mind, is indeed, the soul of All Which Is, concentrated and encapsulated in a physical form. Therefore, it is good to understand that the terminology we use, and while it might vary, it's still imminently the same.

In this way, you will see that God consciousness and the soul are one and the same. It's difficult to conceive of anything without realizing who is conceiving. It is you. It is us. It is each person, collectively or individually, comprehending and understanding one's own existence through the process of self-actualization.

Each entity has but one soul, and that one soul is connected to all other souls through the very aspect of creation itself. Therefore, one soul is also a part of thousands, millions and trillions of souls, but at the same time, all are of the one source. It is the same as if you say that there are a billion candles, and yet, each one burns with the same light. It's no different than sunlight because it too, emerges from the one source.

In the case of candlelight, there is only one light though the candles be many. It's an identical situation with the life force and with souls. We are simply using these terms as reference points to give you some understanding of the levels of consciousness and their connections.

Part of the reason for the entry of spirit onto the physical, is to begin to differentiate spirit energy by means of the physical experience. Obviously, those spirit energies which have chosen the physical birth will have the greatest amount of differentiation regarding their vision of the spiritual experience.

Can you explain this further?

When a soul is born onto your plane, there is an understanding or a self-awareness which comprises certain beliefs and directives, and these determine what may or may not be done during that lifetime. Although it's not imperative that certain possibilities be completed, such preconditions for experience accompany each soul born onto your plane.

It's important to understand also, that the flow of life is constantly trickling over each individual consciousness in this way. As a result, this can change even the prime directives that one brought into this life, so nothing is carved in stone. All activities which occur are perfect for each individual. There is no such thing as a life wasted, or a life which has no sense to it. Whenever you attempt to make common sense out of existence, automatically, you are defeating yourself.

So be aware that existence goes beyond the simple understanding of the physical tenets of being. It is connected more to consciousness which self-realizes on an on-going basis. This gives you a structure and credence. Not only are you a part of That Which Is, but also, you have the ability to differentiate yourself from that oneness as a physical life form, while at the same time, also existing within the unity of that totality.

So we should talk about soul in terms of a consciousness, and speak about soul as coming onto this plane to experience physical consciousness.

Yes, because only you can be conscious. It is you only, who can be conscious. That is all that you can be, is your consciousness. And you must understand that your concept of consciousness in the third dimension exists in the sense that it only happens when the eyes are open and the mind is focussed externally. This, of course, is not necessarily true, but it's the manner in which your philosophers and your scientists have determined the difference. What you must understand is that consciousness goes beyond what you would refer to as physical consciousness.

The true consciousness is the consciousness of That Which Is, and once again, this is a non-specific term because you cannot draw a picture of consciousness. You cannot hold it in a basket and show it to your friends, but you can begin to conceive of what consciousness means to you as an individual. As well, your consciousness is a reflection of That Which Is. Therefore, understand that the consciousness you are now directing while on your plane, is the consciousness which is a part of your own survival mechanism; it keeps you alive, well, and buoyant. Yet, beyond this, the higher aspects of that same consciousness also ensure the continuation and flow of universal energy, and just as important, its comprehension of each one of you at the same time.

So you are saying that there is only the one consciousness which is shared by all, and that self-consciousness can only arise by individuating from that oneness.

Yes, individuating in this way, but there is also an agreement on a much larger scale, that all will accept the physical world as you experience it. Your reality is represented in a way that your consciousness has agreed to observe it, and also, to work within it. Do not forget this.

In other words, our reality here is how we agree to construct it, and how we agree to perceive it. There is an agreement amongst us, as to how we will experience the earth in human form.

Yes.

Going back to what you said regarding the soul being a consciousness, first of all, I am my soul (whatever my soul is), but I am also conscious here in the third dimension and moving through time. Now, when I leave this world, my physical consciousness goes back into whatever greater consciousness I have, or am, which is currently manifesting on this plane.

If you so desire, if you so believe.

Can you provide us with another percept on that?

You must understand that any conceptualization is fine for each individual, and it is something that we would never negate. For you must have some type of benchmark as a gauge, something to determine your place in the infinite capacity of existence. Therefore, this helps to give you a bit of grounding by solidifying it in this way.

On a much larger scale, you will understand that even we, are still in a state of unfolding and growing on an on-going basis. It's part of our contribution to the world to interconnect in this way through the entity David Watson. Yet, for us, oftentimes there are many thousands of energies working together, and at the same time, many of those energies are still focussed in the physical.

It is difficult for you to comprehend how this works on such a thickly layered basis. You see, there is much which is impossible to describe, not because of your limited understanding, but because of our limitations in conveying things to you. It is difficult for us to describe states which exist outside of the physical, because the references to explain them are all non-physical. Yet, how else can we express them except in a physical manner. So we still use concepts of here and there. It's important to understand that as long as you continue to hold onto certain physical ideas, that you will maintain many of the other commonly held beliefs related to physical existence on your plane.

Even if one lets go of those physical beliefs and concepts, you're still saying that your experience is virtually impossible for you to describe, and also incomprehensible for us to grasp because of the impossibility of transferring non-physical referents into a physical terminology that we can understand. So if an individual acts on the premise that he or she is here, now, and is going through his or her life process learning certain things - what happens afterwards?

It continues. Do you not think that we are still learning? Of course we are. We are learning from the process of existing on an on-going basis from moment to moment. Those parts of us which are in a state of constant evolution, those higher parts as you would call them in your terms, are there to help provide certain information to humanity through the entity David. Different energies amongst us come and go to help serve this process. When we interact with you, we are a concept of oneness but there are still other connections that we hold outside of the physical or what you refer to as different dimensions.

In comprehending this connection with different dimensions, we are beginning to fulfil the totality of our own purpose. That totality to which we refer, is something which cannot be comprehended factually within the third dimension.

In the physical world, we receive information provided by the five senses which is further construed by the brain. This gives a structure to our world. The physical body determines how we are going to perceive and how we are going to conceptualize our reality. After death, without a physical body to dictate perception - is that when the mind becomes the creator, and whatever is contained therein, begins to create automatically? Are there only states of being, rather than actual forms in the non-physical worlds?

You must realize that what you are doing in the physical is a state of being as well. It's a creation of the mind - the Great Mind. As a result, your mind which is connected to it, is representing itself in this aspect of itself. Its focus is experienced as your focus, and it's so complete, so realistic, that the physical is the only reality that you can possibly imagine. Therefore, for us even to begin a discussion of what might be experienced outside of the physical, first, you would have to join us. This is not a cop out, as you might put it, it is simply an understanding of the manner in which these expressions can be made.

If we were to connect with you on a non-physical level, our interconnection with you would have nothing to do with speech, nor would it involve what we see, hear or sense, in terms of any of your five senses. You comprehend everything through the conceptualization of using your physical senses which enable you to correspond with your plane of existence. Therefore, it is impossible for anyone to conceive outside of that existence, and subsequently, to be able to comprehend a non-physical state. This is because everything would have to relate in terms of your physical requirements, and thus, describing our state could only be inadequately done.

It's simply a matter of understanding that ours is a different condition which can only be understood once you are in our state. Perhaps the best way for you to grasp it, is by conceiving of it as a dream state where all things are happening at the same time.

So this state we experience in the third dimension is so complete, that we have immense difficulty in envisioning anything beyond the physical or outside of it.

Yes, but this is by direction. This is on purpose. What would be the point of coming onto your plane from spirit, taking a physical form, and then spending your entire existence smirking away as a spirit about the uselessness of a physical existence? You see here, the agreement which became activated and the understanding which occurred at the moment when your physical existence first took place, is that your focus would be entirely directed onto the physical plane. That's the whole point to it. This is what your consciousness is designed to do.

Each spirit is literally a unique biosphere. Each spirit as it is born onto the earth is contained within its own concept of what the world is. There are certain things which are agreed upon, especially because of the use of the five senses which allow you to communicate on your plane quite adequately. Yet, how can you communicate outside of the physical senses? Well, there is much which has been researched at this time, including what is called mind control, hypnosis, and other ways of attempting to explain consciousness.

So perhaps it would be more productive to understand things by using a variety of approaches and terminology.

If you so choose. Do understand that the reason we select particular terminology to explain things, is to allow for the stages of concept formation that you utilize in your dimension. In turn, this gives an individual a sense of progress and accomplishment as understanding arises, while also providing a comprehension of the purpose of existence. For without adapting familiar terminology for this interchange with your dimension, then our descriptions of our existence would not hold any meaning for individuals whatsoever.

Is the physical death process something that we cannot really comprehend from this dimension?

It can be comprehended through past life hypnotherapy. Through such practices, one can journey into past lives and experience the death process as well as the state between physical lives.

Each individual should not exclude any option to reflect consciously on the death state in this manner. To gain insight into what occurs outside of the physical, be aware that nothing can be conceptualized without some point of reference for the conscious physical mind, for it requires familiar ideas and concepts to grasp meaning.

When you are referring to a conscious mind - is that a reference to the third dimensional mind only? Or does the conscious mind become something of a different nature in the non-physical worlds?

We are using it in the terms of third dimensionality. For the conscious earth mind, is part of your survival mechanism. It creates a basis of proof for you to begin to have a stronger faith in the point of your own individual existence. This is what is most important but it's often forgotten in your world.

When one becomes aware of the unity that you are talking about, the unity of all souls and the oneness - does this occur as a natural phenomenon when one is in the non-physical state?

Yes, but it's important to understand that as you view this as a concept, it cannot be relayed to others until they experience it themselves. Therefore, it's more practical for individuals to practice some of the things of which we speak, rather than just reading about them and then saying: I*sn't that interesting.* This is not the purpose of these books, although there will always be some who will pick them up and use them in this manner. As you are aware, it's important that people connect to what is being said.

The manner in which human beings separate everything, is part of their way of cataloguing the physical world. By categorizing, humans have done an excellent job of recording as much as they humanly can about their own physical environment. This is nothing more than glorified stocktaking. In truth, what is most important is not the observation of what occurs, but to understand that which is creating the energy for it to occur. Do you see the difference?

Yes, and as you've said many times, we are the ones who complicate things by our thinking. Even the simplest of concepts, we tend to make them very complicated.

Due to your human nature this is important, because as you are categorizing, it's meaningful to see how one thing correlates to another.

Outside of the physical, there are no ways in which you can particularize and nail things down into this, that, or the other, because your mind no longer has to deal with holding the physical together. Outside of the physical, the mind has an opportunity to open up to the whole self because there are no longer the constraints and inhibitors that physicality requires.

When a soul focuses its consciousness onto the physical plane - is this where the majority of its consciousness resides?

By the very definition of consciousness that's exactly where all of it is. When consciousness resides on the physical plane, physical consciousness is a by-product of the soul. It is born of the soul and the spirit. The soul is not just a pair of eyes; it's your survival kit in the physical. For a soul to exist, it must have conscious sentience and the ability to direct itself. This creates a need for it to direct itself onto the consciousness of the earth plane to experience the physical existence.

Once a soul decides on its future body, be it male, female, healthy, unhealthy, and so on, everything is determined by certain contracts that it has made with itself and other members of its soul group to continue input from a psychological imperative. Understand that physical birth is not only about lessons to be learned on the physical plane.

As the soul comes into a physical body, a certain consciousness is created through the interaction of the soul with the physical. This is you. So in fact, when your soul took on this physical existence, it created a new personality which became you. So you are a newly created physical entity. It is you as this fresh personality of your soul, which develops on the physical plane. In psychological terms, you are a newly developing personality and ego.

Your physical personality and ego will pass through this life and learn certain lessons by having various experiences. At the end of your life, you, as this aspect of your soul, will have reached a point of wisdom which will enable you to return to, and then rejoin with your larger self, and members of your soul group. So what is referred to as a new personality becomes part of a continuous line of creation. Subsequently, you and your energies, will contribute towards creating new personalities also, after rejoining with your greater self or soul.

So there is a group soul or a group consciousness, which individuates into what you refer to as a soul. In turn, that soul incarnates, and takes on a personality, such as ourselves, which is a psychological being which interacts with the earth environment. On the death of the physical body, that personality then returns to the soul, as well as to the group consciousness of the soul family. What happens to the earthly psychological entity when the physical body is no longer alive?

The psychological aspect remains intact, and this is where religion comes into the picture. Many classical religions teach their followers about an afterlife, a place where someone goes. In fact, this is only a part of the truth. The area that many refer to as heaven, a term of reference that we will use for your benefit, is the experience of a state which comprises self-imposed impressions and visions. Therefore, depending upon the beliefs that you hold throughout life, when you pass from the physical into a transitional zone and from there into the non-physical aspects of your psychology - and we challenge you to show us physically where you keep your psychology in life - this psychology remains intact, and creates for itself the visions that it held during life, as to what happens immediately following life.

There are many who espouse this as a philosophy, and we are here to attest to the fact that this is what really happens. Therefore, if an atheist believed during physical life that nothing happens at death, then nothing will happen. That person would lose consciousness and literally disappear, but not be annihilated. Eventually, what would occur is that an understanding would arise that one had lost consciousness. Just because there has been a loss of physical consciousness doesn't deter other activities from occurring. In particular, there might be dreaming, or perhaps out of body travelling - and you cannot get any more out of body than when you are physically dead. Therefore, that consciousness would come back into an understanding that this is what had happened. It would then have an opportunity to rejoin with the other energies from which it had originated, prior to presenting itself into the physical.

Would guides be assisting it?

Yes, you would refer to these energies as guides. They do not have a true physical form in the sense that you would understand it, but they adapt their own energies to the needs of the individual.

So if a departing consciousness needs to see physical forms, the guides will appear in a physical format.

Those who come from Christian beliefs might see cities of clouds containing beautiful, clear, gem-like buildings, and so on. In fact, such places do exist, because it's important for you to understand that the mind as it is creating these in its imagination is in fact producing them on that plane. Therefore, images of heaven do exist in this way.

Yet, there is something that we refer to as being on the other side of heaven, which acknowledges that a consciousness - once it has spent enough time in a comfortable environment - goes through a series of educational situations which once again, will fit into its own personal beliefs. After that, it will perceive that there are new levels to which it can rise. Understand that this is part of an afterlife, and it is unique to each entity.

In your life in the physical, observe your own inner self, and then you can understand how your perceptions work in relationship to that which occurs about you. You will become aware of an inner eye, or something which is observing you, observing life, and this is what you are connecting to, and reconnecting with, at the time of death. You might refer to it as your higher or greater self, which in fact is a connection to your soul which is linked to a group soul. Understand that in this sense, the group soul can also be referred to as being part of the larger aspect of the oneness or That Which Is.

Now, this may sound rather esoteric but in another sense, there is a structure to it. This is important for maintaining the totality of creation. It continues in a constant moment of now, in the sense that your consciousness is here on the physical plane and is developing through the physical experience. Once it has passed through the physical experience and rejoined with the larger mind or the larger soul so to speak, your uniqueness and individuality are not lost, but in fact are expanded and then become part and parcel of a self-recognising entity, one that literally comprehends itself through its own creations.

Yes, and I think that this is where we get confused as humans, because we are so linear in our thinking processes. Again, in order for us to grasp some of these non-physical realities, it's probably easier for us to understand things from our perspective on the earth, and then begin to work backwards rather than the other way around. So, you are saying that the concept of the earth personality will continue, no matter its age at the time of death.

You are not a concept; you are an entity, a soul which has developed to become what you are. This is something which cannot be taken from you. This is part of the ongoing creative aspect of all souls.

So in a future incarnation, basically, the pattern of what one has become in this incarnation will continue on in a different personality of the soul. Is that pattern re-enacted, subconsciously, as to what has been learned and experienced to date?

Due to the energy changes which occur as part of the evolution of the universal mind, there exists the opportunity to maintain patterns of consciousness. So what you consider to be your personality on this plane can continue into another existence and contain a recognition and understanding of this present life as you have lived it. It is this energy which becomes the basis for the next life.

Therefore, a new personality would be created in this sense, but it would be created based on what you already knew about this life, not just the energy levels, but the actual conscious understandings that you would bring forward from your present physical existence.

Whether the new personality is male or female - it doesn't matter?

It's your choice, and it's made before coming onto this plane. Again, these are matters of choice. The affairs of each lifetime are not necessarily chosen prior to coming into this existence. You choose those elements necessary to determine from where the learning will originate during a physical existence.

Which of course, we take back with us.

Not so much that you take back with you, your experience is continually transmitted throughout your physical existence. So in fact, the soul is not something that you come back to, because you are never disconnected from it. The soul has the opportunity to grow with you during the life experience. This is an important consideration. For many believe that the physical experience is separate from the spiritual experience. Whereas the only separation which occurs, is what many have referred to as the illusion of physical existence. It's an illusion in the sense that there has been illusionary information or disinformation, which has been filtered into the social consciousness.

What has been accepted by many in your society and contained within your belief systems is the fact that there is separateness. Alternatively, there exist belief systems which do not embrace separateness but believe in a oneness, such as those of both the indigenous peoples of North and South America. Many of these beliefs have been held since the original times of the first minds upon the earth. There are universal truths available within these philosophies which allow for much in the way of spiritual growth, as well as promoting an understanding of the truths of the physical experience.

Returning to the soul in the physical existence and regarding past lifetimes - have previous lives already occurred, or are they happening simultaneously to this one?

Yes, all lives occur simultaneously. It's a difficult concept to understand. You bring it up because you've heard about it, but you do not understand it. It is hard for anyone within the third dimension to grasp, because your reality only allows for a two dimensional view of life. It's difficult to bring into your consciousness how this might work.

There are those who wrestle with a two dimensional understanding of quantum physics, and so they will theorize back and forth. In truth, what we are speaking about is something that once the mind has achieved a certain degree of elevation by becoming educated regarding its own ability to understand its environment, then the mind will be able to comprehend that it is an integral part of its environment. When you can recognize that you are part of the creative aspect of your own experience, and furthermore, can raise yourself above the consciousness of being in it rather than being of it, then this will provide for a new understanding of the spiritual journey, the awareness that there is no separation.

If a soul had lived a lifetime as a settler in the Caribbean in the late 1700's - would that lifetime be occurring right now? Where you exist there is no time or space - so do all things occur simultaneously?

Yes, to both questions. What needs to be understood is that when you make a change or create an effect in this lifetime, such as a true raisng of your understanding or by changing your viewpoint and behaving differently, you will affect past times as well, for all lives affect all other lives. It cannot be any other way.

As you are aware, these are very difficult concepts to grasp from our perspective.

Yes, they are demanding, and it is also difficult to explain them in words because it winds up as being just another theory in people's minds. Until you can experience this within yourself, it will remain a theory. We can provide certain exercises which will allow the mind to begin to enter into these other states of consciousness, so that you can understand these words more effectively, and actually, observe the images which are attached to them. Words are simply a representation of ideas which are being translated. Words are not always adequate, other than roughly attempting to describe that which is seen or experienced.

Can you provide us with some understanding of your state of consciousness? As you know, here on the physical plane we are very sense bound due to a physical body and its perceptions of reality which define our spatial orientation. Although we have vision and hearing, we are very much connected to language because word concepts form a large part of our consciousness. Can you give us some indication of the soul, as well as the group soul state of consciousness?

As we connect onto the physical plane through the consciousness of the entity David, we become subject to the same rules, regulations and laws, as anyone living in the physical. For us, this is a good thing because it allows for the continual feedback of information back to the larger group, which is a soul group we refer to as The Willows. In fact, it's a soul group of multiple souls.

Our consciousness is individual, and yet, it's collective. Each of us contained within it, has its own understanding of its own uniqueness and being. Furthermore, there has been an agreement to cooperate with each other on a larger scale, as well as collaborating with those who are connected to this group on the earth plane.

Returning to the question regarding our actual experience, we would love to say that we come from an umpteenth dimension and possess the knowledge which will allow the entire world to become enlightened. This is what all hope that we can do, but it is neither our job to enlighten others nor is it the duty of any other. Everyone has the opportunity to become enlightened to this state of consciousness when they can raise their own selves to connect on this level. Part of what we are doing is providing a pathway for understanding that this is possible.

Many, who attempt to envision how the multidimensional process works, might wish to conceive of it in the form of a picture. That image would be structured as a circle within a circle within a circle, within which you arrive at the centre or the base energy of That Which Is. Viewed from the top, it would appear as if you had broken down an old jawbreaker candy, which would exhibit countless multidimensional colours contained within it,

The base energy of each individual thing, each atom and each particle of an atom in the physical universe, is indeed, the same core as that one great consciousness. It's only on the physical level where that consciousness is thought of as being separate, and where different molecules form together to create different types of materials, and ultimately, various types of organisms. This is the physical approach, and it is the one which is most widely accepted in your time.

It's important to understand that although this consciousness can be broken down in the physical, on other levels there is no differentiation. It is difficult to describe the one to the many because the many perceive the one as separate, when in fact the many comprise the one. It's a conundrum in itself and one which is not easily solved.

Looking again at this multiple layering, all which are contained within our soul group emerge from the original source, known as That Which Is or the Great Mystery. For indeed, it is a mystery and it is not meant to be determined or solved on the physical level.

It's what might be called a philosophical element, and the original understanding and basis for the philosophers' stone. The philosophers' stone was that which contained the mind of That Which Is. When the stone was broken and fragmented and individual consciousness came about, That Which Is began to contemplate itself. That Which Is contains all within creation and has the ability to reflect upon its own existence, and this indeed, is what the basis of creation is - that which reflects upon its own existence. This is why the consciousness that all of you hold here at this time, is the very reflection of the beingness about which we are speaking.

On the physical plane, consciousness is structured in the sense that we are located on a planet contained within a physical universe. We see life in a structured manner because of the perceptions and sensations of a physical body. For yourselves, because you're not physical, no such structures exist except for what is created within the soul itself. Is this accurate?

In this sense, yes, there is no physical format. Yet, we are connected to all physical forms at the same time. We are able to manifest through the same, and yet, remain apart from it, allowing a physical form such as David to follow his own path.

When you are not connecting with us in a session such as this one - what do you do? What is your state of experience?

It's important to understand that our particular group is always connected. It is connected to you and to the entity David, and to all the entities on the physical plane who are contributing to its existence. On the non-physical plane, you might ask about our activities. Well, it's not the same as what you do. We do not go shopping and we do not watch television. The best way to describe us is to say that we are continually in a state of evolution. We are part of the cosmic mind which is in a constant state of accumulating experience. You might ask about the types of experience being accumulated. There is no answer to this because it can never be finished, and there can only be the eternal moment of now.

What we are providing by our contact with you, is to furnish an understanding and an assuredness that there is this connection for all beings to That Which Is. An individual is never lost. The fascination of soul with the physical and the third dimension is also part of the comprehension that you are part of the creative process. You must understand that if you did not exist upon your plane, then there would be a void concerning your influence on those about you.

When you begin to embrace your connection to this moment in time, and your involvement with those to whom you are interrelated in this lifetime, all of them would be living different lives had they not met you. It is significant to grasp that there is a reflection of the greater part of existence in the physical existence, and that you are creating your own beingness on a moment to moment basis. At any second you choose, your existence may begin to head in a different direction, once you have made a decision for this to occur.

Which is our free will and choice.

Yes, it's part of the agreement of coming onto the earth plane that free will and choice will become part of the process, but it does not necessarily always have to be a part of the process. Many come onto your plane and feel themselves obliged to do what others say, or to follow what others require of them in order to find acceptance and love. This is an aspect of physical creation too, in which free will is not exercised by an individual. Free will can also be abandoned due to issues of dependency to ensure survival of the physical entity, but no matter what, there still exists a uniqueness regarding each entity's connection to something which is greater than itself.

So perhaps the greatest understanding that can be arrived at by going through this earthly journey is that despite everything, one is always connected to That Which Is.

Yes, it's a reflection of one back to the other. As to the ultimate purpose of this - which is the big question - for that we do not have an answer because the ultimate purpose is different for each individual.

So if one is searching for some understanding and meaning to life, then basically you are saying that it's one's connectivity to the whole. Is this basically the purpose of it all?

Yes, and this is also the purpose of breathing. Respiration is an exchange of energies on all levels. All creatures and all creations have a respiration of sorts. The interaction with the environment substantiates the physical existence of each component. With breathing, there is an element which will allow all creatures to achieve this mindfulness or understanding of a connection to the mind of That Which Is. This universal nexus will begin to seep into the consciousness in a manner which might not be completely understood, but at least the truth of it can be felt.

Would it be possible to provide an activity for going within?

Yes, and we would like to begin with a simple breathing technique which will highlight the nature of breath. Breath is the original exchange of energy which is important beyond all others for human beings. We suggest that you find a quiet place, one where the light is somewhat diminished. That location does not have to be entirely dark, only slightly. An excellent posture for you to take would be what is referred to as the astronaut position - on your back, feet slightly elevated, and hands crossed and placed on the abdomen or by the side of the body.

This breathing exercise is very simple. All you have to do is to breathe in and out, and we recommend that on the in-breath, you take notice of the air entering your body. As you concentrate on the breath as it reaches its peak, there is a moment before the breath must be released. It is at that moment when the true exchange of energy and the connection between the spiritual and the physical is held. This is not a new concept. There are many who already believe this to be the truth and we substantiate this fact. In the moment of that point of stasis, simply concentrate upon it and then let the breath expel. Focus on the breath and not the act of breathing.

Breathing in and out can be done through the nose or with the mouth. It depends on each individual and the amount of congestion within the nasal passages. There is no counting involved with this activity. There is no drawing in, holding, and then exhaling for so many counts. It's a matter of observing the intake of breath, then the moment between inhalation and exhalation, and finally, noticing what is occurring during the out-breath. Also, allow the exhalation to happen naturally without attempting to force the breath from your lungs.

The breathing can be done either through the diaphragm or the chest, depending on which is the most comfortable. You are not disciplining yourself to become a yogi. This activity is geared strictly towards raising the level of consciousness to become aware of what is happening in the moment. It requires between five to ten minutes of your time. If you choose to have music in the background, select quiet passages from composers such as Mozart, Hayden or Verdi. This music can also activate certain changes within the brain, and allow a proper opening of the thymus to release its energies into the body. It can stimulate the opening of the pineal gland as well, a process which is essential to opening the mind to the source to which it is connected.

So during the in-breath, you become aware of the amount of energy that you are taking in, and the feeling of the air which enters your body. While holding the breath, it is important to note what is truly happening in that moment. There is a philosophical question which can be asked at this point: *If I am neither breathing in nor breathing out - then what is it that I am doing at this moment?* It's an instant of exquisite balance, and as we have stated, it can open the pineal gland.

On exhaling, notice where the breath is going. When that breath has fully expired, take the second between that and the next breath, and you have then divided the process into four parts: breathing in, holding, exhaling, and finally, the period before the next inhalation. Those two moments, the time prior to inhalation and the pause before exhalation, are what you are to give the most consideration.

Respiration is an exchange of energies on all levels. The act of breathing will allow you to achieve a focus of mind which can illuminate and expand your consciousness to become more aware of its linkage to That Which Is. The universal awareness will begin to seep into your consciousness and as we have stated, not always in a manner which can be completely understood, but it might be felt instead.

If you carry out this process for five to ten minutes, an exchange of energy will take place which might cause light-headedness. Also, you might feel that your mind is expanding beyond its normal parameters. Try it, it's a good beginning.

Will humanity ever arrive at a consensus as to what constitutes truth?

Be aware that there is an agreement amongst all individuals on your plane as to what is and what isn't true. If enough individuals determine that all should be of a certain belief system, then situations similar to the Spanish Inquisition can arise when all were forced into a particular viewpoint. Those who did not believe and held onto their own views were tortured. In that time, torture was considered to be purgative. It was not carried out to force someone to believe but to coerce people into seeing the truth through their pain. It was an awkward belief system but it's still embraced by some even today. In modern times though, such practices are not carried out collectively within North American society where the concept is considered to be abhorrent.

At the time of the Inquisition, there were those in Spain who practised torture as a way of life. It was justified as being an outcropping of godliness, and thus it was agreed upon by those who considered themselves to be in charge. When a belief system filters down into the social system then it becomes a reality. Therefore, the reality and the agreements which are being held in current times are accords which dictate that mankind will relate through technological means and that the future of humanity has to do with physical gain. By understanding these technological advances, the future of your race - which is considered to be the most important aspect - will continue to evolve. Yes, it's evolutionary - but into a state of what?

There is no answer to this question, because everyone has a different vision. What is happening is that a small number of individuals have already taken control of the world's finances and seized power through money, government and business. These individuals have totally lost their sense of spirit. They have continued dynasties down through the ages. It stretches far back to the end times of Atlantis. These types of beliefs originated from groups like the Sons of the Darkness or Sons of Balial. This has been brought forward not as a mystical tradition, but as a nuts and bolts understanding that those who acquire the greatest number of toys are the winners.

Do these souls attempt to come back into such situations to replay those roles?

Yes, but any soul has the opportunity to take their place. The earth plane is an educational field; it's not the be all and end all. Although the physical experience is wondrous, along with that physical life comes pain and suffering which eventuates in both emotional and physical deterioration, and finally, the pain involved in the obliteration of the physical existence.

As a result, the standard religions which are in control in these times, hold a power base, and declare that the only salvation for the soul is to be good, keep quiet, and act in a sheep like fashion. This has been transmuted into the business world, so it is no longer held only as a religious belief. Pragmatism and cynicism have become the basis for social interaction. Even entertainment through the use of humour, is grounded in this pragmatic cynicism. Such perspectives keep the mind locked onto this plane, thus allowing those in charge to continue to do whatever it is that they need to do.

When a soul takes on a new physical existence, that personality and its experiences during that lifetime could be considered as a new consciousness because it has never existed before. For example, David is a new physical consciousness, I am a new physical consciousness, and when we cross over, each of our personalities will still be intact, and yet, combined with our larger selves. So we will still have a sense of who we were here in the physical, as well as experiencing consciousness as a soul and all of the other personalities which comprise a soul.

Yes, this is true in the way in which you understand it. It is important to comprehend that it's the consciousness of connecting with the soul which provides a true understanding of existence. In that state, nature and beingness become self-explanatory. Metaphorically speaking, it's much the same as when you are looking at certain plants. There is a plant that some refer to as chickens and hens. It's a rounded species, somewhat reminiscent of an artichoke. Once planted, you can observe many smaller versions begin to pop up all around the original. Each of those smaller versions will grow into a full-sized plant. That process continues over and over as the plant spreads throughout the garden. As it extends further and further, it covers an ever increasing amount of ground.

This explanation is much the same as what occurs when a soul recreates itself through itself. A soul group is formed in the same manner. In our example of the chickens and hens - is the original plant any different than the newly created others? From a physical perspective, when you examine any of these plants from a genetic basis, the answer is no. The same DNA structure would exist throughout the original plant, as well as within the smaller ones fruiting about it.

It's the same process when each individualized consciousness is created. Each one will be capable of creating others, while at the same time, maintaining its individual uniqueness within creation. Therefore, every new soul remains a part of the larger process without losing its own consciousness. It doesn't fade, but continues to grow. This growth includes an ever expanding awareness of the states of beingness above and beyond the physical.

So what you refer to as a soul, whenever it takes on a new physical form, a new consciousness is created. When that new consciousness crosses over, you mentioned that it still maintains its physical reference points. After that, it enters into a transition period, where it receives further education by the guides or whatever until it can reach a state of higher awareness. Are there any other analogies that you can use to describe this process? It's difficult for humans to imagine that at death, we will still remain ourselves, and yet, we will be something else as well.

The only you, and any other you, is yourself, whether you be alive physically, or not alive physically. If you are experiencing some difficulty in fully comprehending this concept, another analogy that we suggest, is that to take your own self as the example. The reference to being alive physically or non-physically is a misnomer when referring to true existence and to conscious awareness. As we are separating the physical existence from the non-physical, perhaps this example will help.

Many people consider their existence as solely a physical phenomenon. There is no understanding of a before or an after process, just the time of physical consciousness during that one lifetime on the earth. Be aware though, that there are other planes of awareness, including that one singular plane which is the ultimate, and includes all existence. Know that these states can only be perceived within the physical format. Only in the physical, is there a true separation of awareness from that of the universal consciousness. It's an irony that every soul must form its own opinion of the infinite through its own physical awareness of mortality. Only in this way, can eternity begin to understand itself through the conscious connection which is in play.

I'm beginning to get glimpses of what you are saying but as you are aware, all of it is very difficult to comprehend because of our linear thought processes and the way in which we construct reality in the third dimension. Your analogies, however, do provide some insight. Previously, you referred to spirit guides which are really a part of each individual, and that a person is never really alone due to a connection to a group soul.

Your linear thought processes which construct your reality can be superseded by some of the analogies that we are providing. Your guides are a part of you and exist within you. You are a part of a soul and a group soul. You are never alone, and yet, in the physical all have the perception that they are alone.

The very fact that you physically exist shuts off your consciousness from all other life forms. You will remain in that state until you realize that the same consciousness which is within you is the same consciousness which is within all life forms but without each individualised attitude, so to speak. When one arrives at this realisation, it will be a transformation point.

It is then that you will have raised your level of consciousness to a point where you will be able to appreciate beyond the physical world. It is most difficult for any entity existing within the third dimension, to truly imagine itself outside of that existence because everything that you perceive has been an input stimulus from the external world. When a soul comes onto your plane of consciousness, it cannot help but be affected by what is occurring during its time on the earth. Therefore, it is very important to consider how your consciousness can separate itself from the physical, and simultaneously, be aware of its own physicality.

A technique that you can use is to float over or above a given situation in your imagination. This will provide you with an overview or a generalized perspective. It's the same as if you are looking down from a Good Year blimp. You would be able to see everything as it occurs below without being involved in the activities. By using this technique, it will allow you to survey a situation which is either happening in the present, or one which took place in the past. You can then determine how much a particular event has affected your conscious mind.

Once again, we will mention that you might want to play appropriate music in the background. If you continue to practice this exercise on a regular basis, you will become aware that your mind flows with its own thought processes, and that what you remember is contained within a certain area where all memories related to your own consciousness reside. Also, it's a realization that one thought or event flows into another and by that occurrence, your sense of a time line is created.

Is that the reason why the earth experience is so unique? Is it because it provides the soul with particular understandings which are only available within the physical context? Are such memories and experiences unavailable for a soul on the other planes of existence?

Yes, for you must understand, we are talking about all physical existence and not just experiences related solely to the earth. We are including all other physical life forms within the physical universe in our example. So the perspective of physicality throughout the universe needs to be considered as well.

When a soul creates a new earth personality, is this similar to a dual state of consciousness? Does the soul still remain conscious in its own right within the non-physical, and yet, conscious as a physical being as well? Or is it a situation where the soul has only an overview of the physical human being?

The soul will view the newly created physical being as a spiritual catalyst. Each new personality is a combination of the spiritual aspect of the soul with the physical. Each new earth consciousness, which has been created by a soul, is born with its own unique understanding and abilities. It possesses the same tools as the soul, which enables it also to connect into the same network of information. When we gave the example of the chicken and hens plant which continues to reproduce in order to grow, in the same way, a soul continues to create versions of itself, but those newly created personalities do not differentiate from the soul at birth.

A newly created earth consciousness interacts with the world around it, and that process begins the development of a new personality in its own right. Subsequently, it will start to grow apart from its original energy, or the soul which first came into it. On the other hand, the new earth being will remain in contact with the energy of the soul due to the resonance which remains. So each newly created personality is one and the same as the soul, but it is different as well even though the connection remains intact.

What prompts a soul to create a new earth personality? Is this a part of the co-creation of existence?

Yes, it's a part of the co-creation of existence, and it's the only impetus necessary for the process to take place. Life as you see it, is on-going; it's a constant and continuous event. It never stops, neither on your planet nor in any other part of the universe. It's no different than a male and a female who feel the urge to reproduce and to co-create in the physical. The creative process is never mindless; it's directed and originates from the larger aspect of the need to know. Everything within creation has come into being through a need to know. Initially, the need to know originated from the one omniscience or the universal creativity in itself.

So there is no one director or one individual entity in charge. All entities are collectively connected and intertwined, and that's what creates unity or singularity. This is not a complicated concept for us to explain, but in your dimension it's a difficult idea for you to accept and to internalize. It's as if we are telling you that a finger thinks the same as the head, but at the same time, the finger still maintains its fingerhood.

Can you please explain exactly what a soul is, and precisely where it is?

A soul, as you would see it, is an energy form. It's an energy form and an entity form. A soul has a consciousness. It's not the same as the consciousness that you experience through your physical form, such as when you think about getting out of bed in the morning or how to get ready for work. It's a consciousness which has an awareness of the truth regarding the connection of the physical to the spiritual. The soul comprehends that the two cannot be separated but when they appear to be disconnected; it understands that there is a growth of the spiritual through the physical. The soul is an energy that you can consider to be an aspect of the universal light, the Great Mystery, or in your terminology - a facet of God.

Our reference to God does not consider God to be a singular unit or an entity, but That Which Is. Everything contained within both the physical and the non-physical universe is God. Therefore, you are a part of God.

You can view soul as a seed-bearing plant. It's the original plant which contains the original seeds. Wherever the seeds drop, that's the place where it would reproduce itself but that does not change the structure of the original plant. The soul continues to experience itself through on-going generations which contain those same patterns and dispositions within the physical.

To put it very simply, the soul is a piece of the original energy of creation. When it is planted within the physical world, it begins to realise its potential as a co-creator. It begins to understand that through existence, it can continue to unfold its own beingness both inside and outside of the physical. Therefore, any new personalities that a soul creates, are in fact replicas of itself until those beings become integrated into the life process which has been set into motion.

Each person is connected to, or is part of a soul. The soul is a part of That Which Is, and this includes you. At the end of physical existence, every soul will transmute itself. This will allow it to reproduce itself by creating another individual or another being.

At times, a new personality when it is created is so conscious of itself and its origins, that it does not lose its original wisdom and the energy which accompanied it at birth. That consciousness allows it to deal with the world in a different way than most. Such a being will not hold to a physical identity, believing that it is Bob or Mary Jones, or a citizen linked to a particular address or city. What has occurred is that there has been a realization that the consciousness contained within, is timeless and universal. That consciousness might also recall a past existence to which it has a connection. Examples of such births have been the Nazarene, St. Germaine, Michael, the Bodhisattvas of Buddhism, and the one that you refer to as the Dalai Lama.

The example of the Dalai Lama highlights how a consciousness can come forward from one life to another, without the need to create a new personality in the sense that we have been describing. That consciousness would have a direct purpose and a continuous growth process from one lifetime to the next which is predetermined prior to each reincarnation. That occurrence allows a soul to mature along a direct lineage.

If most of us are newly created individuals, and each of us has been created by our soul, when we cross over after our present lifetime and go thorough the transition period, we become one with the soul which created us. Does the soul then have another impulse to go forward and to create more life to enhance further understanding?

To a degree, but with one exception. One of the decisions taken along the way is for the same soul to have multiple existences. As your consciousness becomes more aware of those particular aspects of existence, it's not as if you become pumped up and full of ego. When you die, your consciousness will expand beyond what you believed you were during this lifetime. The studies that you have undertaken during this life will enable you to contain the consciousness that you now hold and to continue it into another lifetime. All sentient creatures have this opportunity.

There are other possibilities which enable a consciousness to appear in other forms and formats. A consciousness might wish to spend time in another physical form, such as becoming a swamp hog on Venus. This is a conscious experience that you would not understand. It's a life form which lives on methane gas and exists in not much more than a gaseous format. Such a transition would offer no direct relationship from one consciousness (human) to that other (swamp hog), which is more of a feeling of being part of a group consciousness and a collective dynamic; it's a consciousness directly connected to the planet Venus itself.

Yes, it's a difficult concept, but if you want to wrap your mind around it further, consider the planet Venus to be a single conscious being which contains numerous forms of existences in a gaseous format. So in order to understand how this experience within physicality can affect the spirit, a soul might choose to exist in this form.

Is it possible ever to understand these things from our level of consciousness?

It is not just from your level of consciousness that you will experience difficulty understanding these realities. It's from any level of consciousness. Why we refer to it as the Great Mystery, is because the mystery is the mirror itself. It is That Which Is perceiving itself within the mirror. Some belief systems on earth refer to it as the great mirror of consciousness as well. Consciousness takes many forms. There is a consciousness which goes beyond perceiving and being perceived. This is what we are speaking of here.

In other words, even in your state - do you continue to expand and to learn? Is it that no conscious entity can ever arrive at a state of the all-knowing?

Yes, but on the other hand, that's the state within which all exist. The consciousness that you experience and observe in other sentient beings, and even the consciousness of things which appear to be inanimate objects that you don't understand, is still consciousness which is making itself separate from its own original energies, which in this sense you can call the creator. By the very fact of its existence, none can be separate from it. Therefore, that which exists is a part of it. That which does not exist is also a part of it.

Along those same lines of thought, when a soul chooses a very deformed body, parents with AIDS, or to be born into very poor circumstances - isn't that situation chosen and predetermined in the spiritual planes?

Yes, but it is not the same as what the newly created being chooses to do throughout its physical life. Any occurrences which happen during one's life on earth, such as getting a disease - even if that infirmity was acquired at birth - everything occurs to allow that being to understand particular things. Such events are repeated from generation to generation for all to experience the well of human emotions and interactions. Also, and more importantly, it allows for the unfolding of spiritual energy on the physical plane. A soul, no matter what its circumstances, will have an effect on the environment and on the people around it.

Once a new physical personality is created by a soul - does the soul remain in the objective perspective while the personality experiences the subjective?

This is one way to view it. Do understand that a soul does not gravitate towards a particular set of events just because such happenings have not been experienced in former lives. If you think of your own life, you might acknowledge that you have run through the gamut of emotions and do not consider yourself to be a neophyte regarding emotional experience. Do be aware though, that it's your viewpoint concerning any occurrence which will be reflected by your conscious understanding and the universal mind. Therefore, even though you, as a soul, might have had identical experiences in past lifetimes, there exists the opportunity to experience similar events through the perceptions of becoming another physical entity, and therefore, to experience a different view of the world.

No two entities throughout time have ever experienced identical thoughts and reacted in quite the same manner. Similar yes, but not identical. This is the beauty and wonderment of individual creation. So it's important to become aware of how this continuity extends from one lifetime to another. It might happen that in this life that you are disabled or you do not possess sufficient mental acumen to survive or to be successful. That's not the point. By considering your situation and determining if you had good or bad luck, you are conceptualizing the process of living rather than experiencing it.

Remember, it's the moment which is to be experienced. Once the moment has been experienced and lived then you no longer need to worry about the next moment. At that point, you will be living continually within each moment of existence, and your internal dialogue will provide an opportunity for personal growth on the physical plane. You will be able to utilize your consciousness and to share your vision as you have experienced it through your own unique understanding and belief systems.

Previously, you mentioned that some souls do not get caught up in the personality aspects of their physical beingness, and they live more within the universal consciousness. When we begin to transcend our daily state of human consciousness and learn to live more in the moment - is that when we will experience the joy of life and existence, no matter what that existence is?

True, but existence and the experience of existence, as well as its wonderment, are contained within it. For example, we might ask you to find joy in everything you do, but perhaps you'll adopt the attitude that it's an effort to begin to see where the joy resides in what you are doing. It is in the act itself where the joy can be found. This is what we are talking about. The joy is not found in the contemplation of where the joy is. Your state of living in the now can be understood in the same way.

Much of what we are talking about can be found in the broader aspects of Buddhism. It's an understanding of how to utilize the mind to realize itself, and to raise itself to a state of knowing more about what is beyond the physical state. It's difficult to describe because it is outside of the physical realm. The only manner in which we can represent it is by using these terms, and we trust that they serve in providing you with some degree of comprehension.

With your connection to David, and when David enters into trance - is David there with you in soul form?

Always, he is a part of this process; he is not simply a receiver. It took his conscious understanding of what the process is, to allow us to truly communicate in this manner. Therefore, it is important to see that for him and for us, that there is an instant connection of this nature.

And that remains permanent whether he is physically conscious or not conscious?

Yes, and even before his birth onto this plane, there was a connection with this group. Therefore, it is important to see that the separateness which occurs upon physical manifestation is an important aspect, for as you are aware, we are a collective, a combination of experience and affiliated energies that you would refer to as a soul group. In a soul group of this nature, all energies are shared, and there is feeling and understanding of oneness and connectivity. It is important also, for energy to express itself individually, thus creating continuous new experience, input, and information. This is necessary for the on-going evolution of That Which Is.

When referring to such things as the soul, there are many such concepts that we are unable to grasp from this human level of consciousness. Rather than trying to understand everything in terms of our own particular realm of experience, you have said that we don't necessarily have to fathom everything intellectually and it can be done on an emotional level.

Yes, you may put it in this way, but only to a degree. In truth, what you are experiencing is a direct result of your being here, in this time, and in this choice of having consciousness in this moment. It is one thing to say that all exists within the one single moment and that nothing exists outside of it, but that viewpoint creates somewhat of a draconian notion of existence. It's as if all were part and parcel of a preplanned hiccup of the universal energy.

The birth and creation of individual minds, and souls, as you would understand it, is the direct need of That Which Is to experience the totality of its own consciousness which is contained within its own self. Understand that this larger consciousness is not necessarily conscious according to your understanding of consciousness. This is an important consideration. Consciousness is a result of entities undergoing a directed conscious understanding of their own existence. All are the driving force of what you refer to as God, but only in this sense. Once again, it's an unanswerable question: Did God create the physical and did God create man, or did man create God?

That's an interesting concept because we think in terms of our personal consciousness as being a part of the all. From our traditional upbringing, we like to think of a God figure which is self-conscious and apart from what we are, but you continually raise the issue that the God consciousness is what we are.

Yes.

So when you talk in terms of the creator or the creative consciousness, and us becoming co-creators or whatever, that's a part of the universal unfolding and we are never separate from it. Although we are always trying to individuate ourselves from the process in order to understand it, in truth, we are it, we are the God consciousness.

It is important to embrace this concept. In doing so and by realizing the true purpose of physical existence, what will occur for anyone who does this will be the ability to let go of the worries which are connected with physical life, particularly those which are referred to as mortality. This is not to discount what mankind has placed upon the earth when you consider the marvels and miracles herein, such as the advanced manufacturing which produces perfectly crafted vehicles to move about the planet, or flawlessly designed homes and clothing, or masterfully crafted anything that you would ever need. This is referred to as the consumer view of the universe.

As well, all of this is a part of mankind's own efforts within the creative energy, and it is truly a marvel to view that which man has created over the ages. It is important also, to know that man is a creation of That Which Is, and whatever man creates is a direct result of the creative energy of That Which Is. This allows for an understanding that mankind is in a state of constant evolution, moving from an area of conceptualization into the area of creation.

Therefore, consider this understanding not as an intellectual exercise, but as something which may be contemplated to truly begin to identify what is motivating each and every one of you to maintain his or her conscious existence. For all must understand that on one level or another, the physical is only temporary for everyone, but most individuals will live life as if they will never pass to the other side. This is part of their survival mechanism which is an aspect of consciousness allowing one to function safely and cleanly on the physical level.

Regarding terminology, would it be just as correct to refer to the soul as the superconscious?

No, because the superconscious is the survival mechanism of the soul or the spirit on the physical level. The superconscious is what others have referred to in the past as the unconscious or subconscious. It incorporates all of that plus the spiritual aspects of existence. It's not necessarily a bigger and smarter version of you. It is more a natural version of you which expresses itself automatically on the physical plane to ensure your on-going survival during your conscious travels in the physical.

Therefore, the superconscious is that which holds all memories and all thoughts of things past, and it contains tremendous reserves regarding the understanding of existence. Through its application, the superconscious brings forth automatic behaviour systems as well as what you might call a balanced physical self. It's important to understand that the superconscious must communicate with the conscious mind. The conscious mind can be viewed as the lens of the mind, and the unconscious or super conscious can be regarded as the operator of the body and the mind. When you refer to the higher consciousness or soul aspect, there are many terms which are used synonymously.

Also, during your time in the physical, if you can take the position that you have already done everything in your life which has to do with completing this lifetime, then you can take time and remove yourself from this cycle of birth and death, and also free yourself from worry. In regards to spiritual matters, you will be able to turn to the aspects of your development as an individual who exists on the physical plane.

You are completing your life on a day to day basis. It is unfolding for you on a conscious level. What we are saying when we suggest that you consider yourself to have passed over, is not that your life has already been lived, but if you can live your life as if you have already passed from it, then you may get the greatest joy out of each moment of existence. You will no longer have to worry about living your life because all you have to do is to go with the flow of your life. If you live your life in this way, you begin to leave regrets behind for you will no longer leave things out of your life that you would regret later.

What about those who believe that things they have done during this short lifetime, will result in eternal fire and damnation?

Those on your plane are taught these particular belief systems through their own religious bias and backgrounds. At this time, such views are held by approximately twenty-three percent of the earth's population. It is important for those who hold such beliefs, to begin to explore other visions regarding their own existence. For it is a difficult and arduous journey for some, to let go of their old belief systems which were ingrained from early childhood and accepted due to the teachings of their religions.

We do not suggest that people begin to eliminate these beliefs, but instead, begin to evaluate their validity in relationship to what they already subjectively and intuitively know about the truths of their own existence. This is the purpose of physical life, so that you may take your subjective vision of your own experience, and begin to apply it towards the larger picture of reality or non-reality as it is being presented by the world about you.

What about the belief in karma or predestined experiences?

Regarding the intervention of the fates for those who believe in karma and its retribution, these beliefs have been passed down so that people will live their lives in fear and trembling, or used as an excuse to say that something has been God's will and part of a divine plan. There is no ultimate plan, except for the growth and the continuation of the life process on the physical.

On the spiritual levels, it's another matter. At times, this becomes difficult for us to express. We can offer only guidelines because each entity experiences both the physical and the non-physical in a different manner. Regarding destiny, understand that the physical body chosen is the one which will offer certain advantages and disadvantages in life. This allows souls to have a physical experience which permits them to gain direction and to understand the truths of physicality.

A physical body is not something that a spirit slips in and out of, just like a pair of shoes. Physicality dictates that once the integration of body and soul takes place, spirit becomes whole within its physicality for the duration of that body's existence. When a soul first arrives on the earth, there are certain visions that it would like to have unfold for itself or things intended for resolution throughout that life. It could be something like how to learn to love oneself, or how to interrelate in certain ways with other beings.

While living in the physical, there are simple, basic truths which will add value once they are understood on a spiritual level. What occurs for some, however, is despite the best of intentions, before they know it, other activities challenge flexibility making it difficult to stay on track to discover one's intended direction. Although each lifetime is a new experience, every aspect is not necessarily decided before it begins. That would not allow for originality or growth on an individual basis.

So each soul carries a mission statement concerning what it would like to accomplish. Does this get waylaid sometimes because of competing interests?

Correct.

There is a belief which is prevalent in many new age circles, that for a spiritual entity, it's a privilege to have a physical body, and that there are not enough human bodies to go around. Is this a misconception?

It's made up by those who have physical bodies (ha, ha). The truth of the matter is that spirit is everywhere. Spirit is everything. There is nothing outside of spirit. Everything is contained within it. This is what we mean when we speak about the omniverse, and yet, within it, is the containment of all levels of existence and understanding, even what you refer to as different dimensions.

When you ask specifically about the energies of individuals, it's important to see that as spirit manifests in the physical, it expresses itself in all aspects of the physical, such as in the wavelengths of the light emitted by the stars. Spirit is evident in the movement of single-celled creations existing in the darkest corners of the world, or in the depths of the oceans, or in the hottest deserts where life thrives. Spirit is alive also, where life does not flourish, and even on other planets which are alive with the changes that physicality impacts upon them. Outer space - which you consider to be a vacuum - is not empty; it's a combination of different wavelengths such as radiation and sound which are not carried by any atmosphere, but by interdimensional vibrations which also move throughout the physical universe. All things contain the energy of life and existence.

Therefore, you can't say that a spirit is waiting to get into a physical body. It will occur within its own time frame. We ask you with some humour - what is so great about physical existence on your planet anyway? What makes it superior to existing on planets in other parts of the universe? All of that has yet to be explored by humanity. There are other forms of existence on other planets and in different dimensions. There are other means to sense existence, and ways of being which are outside of the physical experience. Other forms of existence are not inferior or superior, but part of a totality which includes your own individual experience. Realize that what you taste during this lifetime is one nth, of one nth, of one nth, of a degree of the totality of your own potential in the light of what exists within creation.

You have noted that one particular life on earth reflects only one aspect of a soul's total beingness. Is this due to the fact that our higher state or the superconscious part of the self is a highly ethical being? What about entities such as the ones who perpetrated the attack on the World Trade Centre on September 11, 2001?

Each of those entities believed it was that higher aspect or moral being which was behind their actions. Let's look at what can happen to man's best friend - the dog. All dogs have the same basic nature, which is to be with mankind. They perform such duties as hunting, and also provide love without asking for much in return. Dogs can be taught to kill each other, to maim, and to destroy human beings. Such animals are trying to serve their masters, even though their humans have twisted views. By performing those acts, the dogs are attempting to get the type of attention required to make them feel loved and accepted.

It's the same idea with those who committed the acts of terrorism, and the situation is similar. We are not referring to them as dogs in any sense, for dogs and humans are of a different vibrational level. Those who planned these acts were dealing with issues of power and furthering their own agendas. Those who carried out their plans were the followers. They were the one's who believed that they would receive some form of benefit by sacrificing their lives, and going against the basic tenets of human existence. Twisted as it might seem from your point of view, they believed that they were fulfilling their destiny and receiving succour from their superiors. Do understand that on your plane there are cycles. As part of these cycles, certain individuals will become available at key points to create shifts, especially in global terms.

It is my understanding that a soul can occupy more than one physical body simultaneously. Is it possible to be connected to other physical life through one's soul?

The answer is yes, according to the way in which you are interpreting it, but don't get too excited about the concept. There is not always a conscious understanding of this reality. For instance, let's take you for example. Contained within you, personally, is the major source of your focus on this plane. On the other hand, you are connected also to a kimono dragon and a calico cat in the Hebrides. Additionally, you are associated with a redwood tree which is currently growing in Northern California. These are areas where your consciousness shares experiences on your plane. It's the method by which a soul works within multiple consciousness in the physical.

Having this knowledge allows you within a contemplative moment, to be able to experience awareness apart from the one that you so fastidiously cultivate on a daily basis. This will create for you an opportunity for harmony and synchronization with other life forms. It will give you a deeper appreciation of the expanse of your consciousness which can focus on another aspect. This will allow for a truer balance within you.

Many humans today hold a similar process of connectivity to other life forms. It's important to realise also, that more than one soul can occupy one physical body. There can be two, or even three souls occupying one physical vehicle and experiencing a singularity of consciousness through that mind. From this example, you can see how a spirit does not have to be connected solely on a one to one basis in the physical, which allows for a more unique internal experience through the same process.

I was reviewing your references to a soul and its physical personality, and I still find it confusing.

This confusion is created because you think in a logical and linear manner, such as when you think of here and there. For perception on the physical level, there has to be some form of flow chart in order to process information.

We shall attempt to place it in terms of your requirements. Consider the soul as layers. These are layers from the inside out. Imagine a large onion which has a seed contained within its middle. This epicentre contains the energy for all new onion growth. This is the same as you, here, at this time. Surrounding you, however, is the energy of the onion itself. This can be referred to as the soul. Consider the earth to be that which the soul comes from, and that from which the onion grows and takes its sustenance. Using our frame of reference, you may consider the earth to be the greater soul. This does not preclude that the earth is not part of a larger system, which indeed it is, because it works within that system, not only to maintain the integrity of itself, but of the system as well. This is the same interconnection. That's the best way we can explain it,

Can we explore more of what the soul is as a higher entity and what constitutes the superconscious state? Is the soul always conscious within its own right, even though it is embodied in one or more physical personalities?

Once a soul decides on its future body, be it male or female, healthy, unhealthy, and so on, all of it is determined by certain contracts that it has made with itself and other members of its soul group. This is to continue gaining input from the psychological aspects of physical existence and not just to learn lessons on the physical plane.

As the soul comes into a physical body, a certain consciousness is created through the interaction of the soul within the physical. This is referred to as the physical being. So in fact, your soul created a new personality which became you when your soul took on this physical existence. It is this new physical entity which develops on the physical plane. In psychological terms, you are a newly developing personality and centre of consciousness.

Your personality will pass through this life and learn certain lessons by having various experiences. At the end of your life, you will have reached a point of wisdom which will enable you to return to, and then integrate with your soul and members of your soul group. So what is referred to as a soul becomes a part of a continuous line of creation. Subsequently, once you intermix consciously with your soul or greater self after your current physical life, in a subsequent lifetime, part of your current energy might contribute towards bringing another personality into existence.

The best way to explain it, is to note what happens when an energy in its completeness on the physical plane passes into spirit. It combines with its original energy and the energy of the original energies of all of its predecessors, and the sequence of events. There is continuity and a homecoming. Once connected with these others, if there is the choice to reactivate that energy on the physical plane, only part of the energy will return to the physical.

It's as if you had two containers of water with one being larger than the other, and you take the smaller container and dump it into the bigger one. All of the water will mix together. Then, if you so choose, you might pour out water from that larger container into three smaller ones. Each of the three new containers would hold a small part of the original. This is much the same as what happens with creatures born onto the earth. There is always plenty of energy willing to come onto your plane. It's only a matter of how that energy will be directed.

Are certain experiences which cause suffering predetermined?

All entities suffer in the physical. There is emotional pain and physical pain. Physical life is not considered to be a walk in the park. Part of physical experience includes the opportunity for a spirit to develop its own finer sense of limitations. Certain behaviours or actions will be tempered by their outcomes. This is what the physical existence will do, particularly the experience of the pain which accompanies the consequences of certain actions. Sometimes, pain is a moderating agent and on other occasions, it serves as an aversion. Pain is either the basis for growth or aversion. Some will utilise pain to propel them forward. As a result, they become more spiritually adept because they learn to adapt to whatever is occurring around them.

The determination of all that you experience throughout a lifetime comes specifically from the decision to enter into a physical life form. It's this physical entity that you refer to as alive, but for many humans, the spirit within is not seen as alive although spirit is more alive than life itself. For all life is comprised of spirit. Spirit is the energy which animates the flesh. It's a very complex series of interactions which allow a soul the energy to materialize and manifest on your plane.

The decision to enter the earth plane is a collective one. Does God make that call or do you? In fact, you are God and God is you, but the question remains - who sent whom? The truth is that it does not matter. What is important is the life experience, and that which is encountered during the time frame of a personality in a sentient form.

Do you choose to be with certain individuals? Yes, indeed. There are combinations of agreements among souls before arriving on the physical plane. It has already been accepted who will be the parents, the children, brothers, sisters, spouses, friends, neighbours, and so forth. It is not done in the sense that it has all been preset, as if all concerned were cast in a large, Broadway musical. You do not choose the outcomes. You chose to be in your body. As your acceptance of that fact becomes more complete, then the opportunity for your own advancement becomes more enhanced.

It is not as if prior to taking a bodily form, you decided to get cut and have salt poured into your wounds. Nor does it occur that a supreme being would do the same. We are speaking metaphorically. In fact, what occurs is the opportunity for complete freedom of action and activity following each event, especially if it has been life changing for an individual. Then it's a matter of how a person reacts and grows from the circumstances as events become incorporated into his or her life's process. It's not just your life's process, but the manner in which each person affects the lives of those around them, including those you have known in life who have become non-physical and are now on the spiritual plane. Be aware that connectivity occurs on all levels.

There is an understanding that it is not just the lessons of the individual from his or her own perspective, but it's the lessons of the interactions with the environment and with those beings who live within your immediate sphere. Perhaps you meet someone when you are downtown who asks you for a dollar. As you give money to that person, maybe it changes your views concerning the homeless because you see within that individual a connection to your own self. This is the manner in which that person was intended to affect your life. It might have created far more of an impact than even the person with whom you have chosen to live and to partner with during this lifetime.

There is no uniformity as to what is important and unimportant when it comes to each individual's purpose in the physical. Insofar as the growth of each person into a distinct personality who interacts with others on your plane, the ultimate goal is to increase conscious awareness of your own state of being. This is so you may grow beyond those simple day to day aspects concerned with earning a living and attempting to get ahead. Although these are a part of the process, they are not the essence of it.

The essence is to be able to look back and to determine exactly what is projecting the picture onto the screen of everything that you are enacting. This is the best way that we can describe it. As you do this, you will begin to see that certain actions and activities in life begin to unfold. These will begin to fan out in a logical manner which will direct you towards certain accomplishments during your lifetime's experiences. If you think about the extremely difficult individuals you have encountered in your life, people for whom others cannot discover any active graces or purpose, even these people have a great effect on the overall pattern of existence. Such individuals serve as an example of what not to do. Others, who exist in a state of dire need, are there to help test and create the essence of love and compassion within others, as well as to highlight how one can become the product of one's own decisions.

So your arrival upon the earth plane is not meant to be purposefully aimed towards or against other individuals, but it is one to be understood and directed once the acceptance of it has occurred. This will create an overall connection to the collective consciousness, rather than solely to individualistic experience.

Are one's experiences planned before each life?

It is important to understand that each individual creates his or her reality from moment to moment. So yes, there is a decision made by an entity, or energy, or spirit, to enter into the physical and experience the true human birth in this way. Thus, there is the decision to enter into life. Then there is the decision which is made along the way as to how to act and react to life's situations. An individual, who makes a decision in one moment, might be able in another moment to look back and say: *How could I have ever made that decision?*

All of you have chosen to come to the earth to experience a physical life. You are wondering if you chose your experiences prior to birth. It's the same as saying that you chose a book or a script and when you arrived here, you not only read the book but became a character in it. No, life doesn't quite work in this manner. If everything were predestined and prearranged, then there would be neither opportunities for alternative movement within life nor openings for growth. Physical existence would merely be an occasion to become an excellent actor by playing a prearranged part.

Is there a preapproval process regarding a particular physical life that a soul wants to experience?

There is no one to approve or to disapprove, and this is not what happens. What occurs is that a decision is made for actual contacts, including the direction for a place and time of birth, parents, and so on. You do not arrive with a life script in your hand which will unfold through its own volition. Before birth, souls will make agreements to have relationships with each other while passing through the physical. As you are aware, many souls incarnate together in groups, and subsequently, they will have similar energies about them while physically alive. There are no prior contracts written in triplicate. There are agreements that entities will meet and cross paths, which will allow them to share certain experiences at particular junctures. Such meetings can become the basis for newly creative experiences.

How will you know when it happens? Be aware of the familiarity of energies. When you meet certain people, you can't necessarily say that you were destined to meet. It's not as if two spirits came to earth with a prior arrangement to meet for a coffee at the corner of 42nd and Vine on July 1st, in such and such a year. What happens is that you grow and become more intuitive in the physical, and therefore, become more attuned to how the spiritual and physical work together. Your intuition will draw you towards those who hold an equivalent energetic basis, people of similar degrees of progress in life.

There is a universal part of you, a universal self which is all-knowing. At times, you will meet someone and share what you need to share. It's the same when others share things with you. It's as if you are somewhere, and suddenly, a key is turned and information flows forth for the advantage of either yourself or others. It's a natural ability that all entities hold, and in particular, a proficiency of those who are on a spiritual path which is leading them away from believing that everything is based in the physical.

Is there a soul group which determines what we are going to do in this life?

Not in this way, and as we have indicated, there are contracts which individuals agree to, but these contracts are not related to what you are going to do, but what you are going to learn and what you are going to contribute. How you learn it and how you give, is a matter of your own inventiveness and your individual right of creation during the life process itself. This is in combination with a variety of energies which you may refer to as your spirit guides, your original energies, or your soul group, whatever is important to you. So be aware that you are always surrounded by love.

So when entering into the physical state to determine what your contracts are, you are surrounded by the other energies with which you resonate, not only in this time, but in all times. When it comes to determining what your contracts are, or what is needed to be done, there is a soul wish which comes from the individual as to what is required from each particular experience into which one enters.

Usually, this includes simple aspects rather than complicated ones, including the ability to learn to love oneself or the capacity to learn to be kind to another, or to be tolerant, and so on. These are simple contracts, and therefore, that which is necessary for the progress of the soul. Also, there is a necessity for the soul to reconnect with the universal mind, and thereby, refresh itself and become part of a higher consciousness outside of the physical.

Contracts are agreements to have certain connections occur during the physical life span, so that certain learning will be revealed consciously. It's not as if you know everything before you come here. We wish to impress this upon you. Many would question this by wondering why they are so smart in the spirit and so stupid in the physical. The fact is that there is no such thing as smart or stupid when it comes to physical or spiritual life.

Basically, it's a matter of consciously unravelling the awareness of the totality of That Which Is. This does not come quickly or in one lifetime. Those who are now beginning to enjoy such rewards have lived many lifetimes in many times and places, and had many questions answered.

How do we discover our soul wish?

It is up to each individual to undergo one's own process to have it revealed. As you go through that experience of contemplation, you begin to understand some of the things that you are learning, and new ways to behave and to act. Only on the physical plane can certain things be enacted. So on returning to the spiritual, along with the love which was experienced, any new learning will be taken to heart.

I have a question about animals and the soul. Recently, we lost a cat through tragic circumstances and I was wondering about the soul of an animal - does it go back to a concept of a group soul?

As you understand, the concept of a soul is only a reference point from which to proceed for the purposes of this conversation. Most people understand the soul of a human being to be individuated, and so they tend to think about animals in the same manner. Although each creature has its own particular disposition on your plane, the souls of animals are part of an overall consciousness, as is the case with all consciousness. This overall consciousness, shares, reflects, and realises its own totality through its individual creatures, such as dogs, cats, horses, snakes, spiders, and whatever the case might be. Within every individual creation, exists the reflection of the whole.

Animals operate under different circumstances than humans when entering and leaving the physical. The malleability of the overall consciousness does not discriminate when taking the form of an animal, whether it be a chipmunk, a cat, or a tree. The universal mind has a need to perceive through all existence, including animals. As all life must continue, the process is irreversible and life always continues to self-perpetuate. The soul of a human is a part of the larger dynamic as well.

So there is a difference when you are considering the idea of souls and the animal world. There seems to be a certain naiveté and innocence which is connected to each creature. There is no act of evil carried out by any animal. By projecting human values onto the natural order, only humanity attaches a concept of evil to animal behaviour by deeming any of their actions to be covert, negative or wicked.

Is there a heavenly state for animals?

Yes, in one sense. They do return to the original spirit form. In fact, one of the gifts of creation is not only an awareness of the larger whole, but more important, the awareness of the individual aspects of existence. Therefore, animals will return to a heavenly state and remain more or less in a pattern familiar to those with whom they were connected. We are speaking specifically about those you would call domestic pets. In many cases, they are subject to the same rules and regulations as those of humans, so they can understand the connection of the spirit to the physical. After their passing, animals can appear to their masters and to those who looked after them during physical existence.

So they still maintain their physical form in spirit?

It's a projection of their physical form. You must understand that form is the way that a human mind receives information for something to appear real on your plane. Therefore, a connection with your pet is the same as a link to a close member of your family or a friend. There is something which goes beyond the physical and remains with both parties for eternity. It's a part of the connectivity and growth pattern of the universe. As well, it's a continuation of the universal understanding of emotional growth.

With the cat that we lost - where is that animal now? Does it still exist in another form?

What exists is the connective spark. This connective spark is the true connection of this creature to your plane. In the first place, its attraction into your own heart and home was also a part of your attraction into its heart and home. A cat can never be a pet; it can only be a companion, and unlike other creatures can never be owned. That is one of the qualities which attract people to cats in the first place.

What has happened to your pet? Give yourself a quiet moment at home and recall your memory of this cat. Then call this animal to you in spirit form. Simply repeat its name in your mind. Send it the same affection and love that you had always given it in life, that is, embrace the feeling of comfort and the exchange of energy which always occurred when you touched him. This will attract the essence of this cat to you. It has not really left you. It was your cat and therefore, this animal will remain connected to you in this way.

There is also another bond that you had with this animal. What is important for you to know is that its spirit, in essence, was connected to the energy of your deceased maternal grandfather. His continuing connection to you on the physical plane was through this cat. As a part of his spiritual revelation, a choice was made to exist in that format.

In many instances, animals can be thought of as fragmented spirits of consciousness in a similar manner as human beings are fragments of a greater soul. In the case of your cat, it was a connection for you and your family to your maternal grandfather. There was the understanding that here was one who would watch over and be a presence with which you could be comfortable. Whilst you might consider the cat's passing to be tragic, it was also a natural occurrence, as there was a need for it to complete its energy on the spirit plane and thus remove its essence from your world at that time. Part of what happened was to reflect energetically in your own life, your need to cope with the idea of loss. For there was no loss to the animal and its consciousness, because it reunited with the oneness and the totality of its being.

Was it meant to be that the cat left at that time and in that manner?

No, it was not meant to be, because nothing is preordained. All is open to randomness. The events which led up to his demise or the manner of his passing, was the means chosen to depart the physical existence and to leave lessons for those who remained behind. As was his habit in life, your grandfather was one to speak of practical lessons and this occurred once again through his departure via the cat. Don't consider only the physical manner of this animal's leaving, but examine the emotional impact and your enhanced understanding of the continuity of existence. No matter how unnatural this might seem, it's important to understand the naturalness of the situation and that everything which is in the physical crosses to the spiritual at some point.

Particularly for yourself, it helped to bring back into your consciousness, the impact, the immensity, and also the fineness of the line between physical and spiritual existence. Not that you needed a refresher in this, and certainly not under those circumstances but it was more to give you cause for reflection. For in truth, another's loss cannot be measured or gauged by anyone except the individual who has suffered the privation.

Can souls incarnate into animals?

An excarnate human consciousness cannot return directly into an animal form. This is what is known as the transmigration of a soul, or the reincarnation into an animal form rather than returning to a human one. These are theories which have arisen due to the limitations of physical consciousness.

Will you comment on animal consciousness?

It's important to consider the aspects of consciousness which come into these creatures. There must always be some form of deliberative aspect in an animal which allows it to react to the physical environment. An animal requires the proper tools to remain in a state of reactivity throughout its normal life cycle. Animal existence provides a basis for the greater understanding and wisdom of all life as it continues to evolve.

So what is the purpose of self-consciousness?

Simply put, it's the joy of existence. It's an understanding that the uniqueness of each physical consciousness that the soul will pass through will bring a new vision, a different understanding, or an alternative facet. It's as if you are polishing an exquisite jewel. Each time that the stone passes through a lifetime, more depth becomes noticeable as more cuts and polish are added. The essential quality of the jewel never changes. The stone remains a diamond, a sapphire, or whatever. What you are viewing is the total cut and that is what influences its beauty and radiance.

So it's the joys of existence and experience which add to our overall consciousness. Are you saying that no matter what we go through be it good or bad, that everything adds to the totality of our consciousness?

It's the knowing. Be aware that there is an emotional attachment to it as well. Love and joy reflect everything within creation. It's as if there is a celestial song which passes through all states of existence. It's a vibration which connects everything on a deeper level. When you can tune into it, you will find yourself in an altered state of consciousness, whereby, you will allow yourself to be only in that moment. It doesn't matter what that moment is, because it is only in the moment that you really exist.

All of that energy you expend when you look back to see what has been, or when you look ahead to examine what could be, does not exist within the moment that you are experiencing. Just as important, what was, also does not exist within the moment you are experiencing. We are speaking of the events themselves and not the psychological impacts or implications.

So the only time you can exist is within the one moment. It's the same moment that we are speaking of, when we ask you to become aware of the moment in-between inhaling and exhaling, or the systole and the diastole. It's that same moment which is created in the universal understanding of That Which Is or the Great Mystery. There is only one time, one moment, and one existence. You are experiencing it now. You cannot experience it at any other time but in the moment.

If you think about how you are experiencing that moment, then you are not experiencing it. If you are wondering how to experience it, you are certainly not experiencing it. If you question the now in relation to your thinking processes, because of a concern that your existence in the now might eliminate your need for consciousness, again, drop this consideration. You must begin to truly appreciate that in the moment all is one, because in the moment, the one is realising itself. Each individual, every aspect, and each atomic particle, can indeed realise its own self through the very nature of its own existence, that is, in a universal state of love and joyousness. From that perspective, you can realise your oneness with all of creation.

- 4 -

NON-PHYSICALS

Do angels really exist?

Angels are a creation of humans due to the fact that humanity has placed its faith in angels. Angels portray a combined physical-spiritual representation of the universal mind or the Godhead. Angels have been spoken of in many religions and philosophies, and not just by Christians. Sometimes, they are thought of as sages, holy people, or ascended Masters. The creation of angels has arisen from an understanding that there is a transitional zone between the physical and the Godhead. There is a belief that angels represent this transition zone, and that this place of transit makes it unnecessary for a human consciousness once it has arrived at a certain degree of understanding, to return to the earth in a physical form. There is also the belief that angels will interact with those on your plane.

Some individuals view themselves to be in such a state of unworthiness, it becomes their conviction that only through heavenly intervention by beings such as angels, can their unworthiness be assuaged and balanced. In truth, there is no universal deity which holds people unworthy, only individuals themselves can arrive at that conclusion. A state of unworthiness is a state which people create for themselves. It's a belief that their individual circumstances, or the perceived attributes of another, violates their own sense of worth on the earth plane. Those who suffer from these beliefs base their self-importance on what value they are to others, or how others respond to them. They relinquish their individuality and sacrifice themselves for recognition on a social basis.

There are different interpretations of angels. Angels are what we will refer to as a thought collective. For example, people think of the archangel Michael. This is part of a legend which has been passed down from generation to generation. Many people have prayed to this angel. On the physical plane, when mind forms are focussed on a certain belief, it becomes a reality and takes form through the creative process. The mind is a creation of That Which Is or what some refer to as God. Therefore, everything which is a creation of God has the opportunity to have Godlike abilities and can create other things such as angels. This is why angels have been construed as humanlike, rather than having the form of something which existed prior to the creation of humanity.

Nevertheless, this does not prevent angels from appearing to mankind as figures of great strength. Angels as you know them have arisen from Christianity and the Judaic beliefs, whereby, angels were thought to have been created from the God energy. Since those earlier times, angels have become an established belief system, and subsequently, have become connected to people on the physical plane. For those on the earth, angels create a system of both support and belief. If one totally believes in the existence of angels, and furthermore, has a total emotional commitment to the concept, then angels will appear and conversations can take place.

In other words, it's the belief in such beings which makes them real. In the same way, this is how other entities of a similar nature exist. It's a result of that which has been concentrated upon by humans over a period of time, which in turn, creates the manifestation.

So angels aren't actually souls, but are created by the belief systems of mankind. If someone wants to see an angel and has the belief and the emotion - would the appearance of an angel be a creation of someone's own mind, or actually an entity from another dimension?

There are certain areas in the physical which hold particular energies. All of the elements hold energy. There are angelic apparitions in the form of water and tree sprites, nymphs, and numerous others. Nymphs have arisen through pagan beliefs, using the terminology of Christians. Once again, these are the representations of the same energies because that which humankind's collective consciousness has created indeed is real.

Now, as to the question of who creates these entities - is it humanity or the creative force? You must realise that mankind is created by mankind from one generation to the next. This does not make one generation any less valid than the one before it. Therefore, it's important to understand that because ethereal beings such as angels are created by the minds and the collective consciousness of humanity, it's no different than if they had been created by the creative energy.

From that perspective, nothing is separate, not one thing from the other. There is no God which has an ego, which takes a position, and then worries about who created what. It's all a part of the creative process which is the on-going generative process of existence. So these beings are not of another dimension, but instead, you should consider them to be another level of consciousness. Consciousness does not require a dimension so don't get confused.

Angels are a concentration of spirit or the original energy, which is then quantified and focussed through the physical needs of someone on the physical plane. Understand that all individuals are spirit. Sometimes, when a person becomes stuck and requires reconnecting, or perhaps a jarring to help them to realize or reunite with their own path, it can create the necessity for contact with what are referred to as angels. These will be representations of an energy form which becomes focussed due to an intense emotional need at that moment in time. These energies will materialize in the form that you recognize as angels.

Even though angels appear to originate from a human base, it's not as if a human thinks about creating an angel. An angel is the result of the energy being expended at that time, allowing that energy to direct itself into a format which would benefit that person in need.

Angels, in the form you see them represented today, were created in Phoenicia. They are a result of humankind's need to fly, such as the legend of Ichorus when he flew too close to the sun and his wings melted. This story was relayed to the Greeks from the Phoenicians.

These legends all originate from the same source, which is the legend of Gilgamesh who was given the gift of immortality. He did not earn this gift but quested for it. Ultimately, he refused the quest and he refused the gift. He understood that the greatest gift was his own consciousness, plus the fact that he existed on the physical plane in a transitory manner which allowed him to become one with the totality and the creative energy which is the progenitor of all life.

Depicting angels with wings was the result of observing birds. It was assumed that at some stage, humankind in its state of spiritual evolution would reach a point of being able to fly like a bird. In beliefs such as Catholicism, there had been observations of men which had flown but this was considered to be an oddity rather than a miracle. The angel aspect in the manner of flying is a physical representation of raising the individual in bodily form above the earth plane.

Anthropologically speaking, this is the best way to describe it. It represented a need to rise above the mundane, and was described crudely as the ability to sprout wings. In time, angels became adapted into other belief systems, including those of the Greeks and more importantly, the Romans who had a great influence on Christianity, one of the greatest that any nation had on a religion of the earth.

Seraphim, or angels resembling Cupid, were attached to Roman mythology. When individuals converted to Christianity, these visions were brought with them and transferred in that manner. Angels were created by those who felt that they would be unable to have direct contact with the creative force, as well as by humans who felt that their power had been stolen or removed. This was to enable mankind through its connection to angels, to begin to raise its level of consciousness and to allow for a greater comprehension of one's own particular situation in life.

Are there such things as guardian angels?

These are closer to guides and will manifest to an individual in the most acceptable form. If you existed in another society, the concept of a guardian angel, a guardian, or a guardian guide, might not take the form of an angel but rather another type of entity which is a product of that society. Don't think that because things are created in this manner that they are invalid. In fact, just because they originated as a result of the collective consciousness of mankind, doesn't mean that they don't have as much validity as anything else in creation.

Guardian angels do not guard as much as they act as additional radar for your journey, allowing you more awareness of what is taking place around you. They assist also in keeping the line open between your conscious self and your spirit. In other words, allowing the process of complete experience to unfold in each individual. They do not hang around as advisors, although those who have a wish to use them in this manner may have the opportunity to receive information from them.

These guardians work in much the same way as you would consider us to be working. They do not jump in and volunteer information. In fact, it is only when they are acknowledged that the information will begin to flow through the individual who requested this connection.

The connection must be preceded by questioning. It is always important to ask these guardians questions, and then await the answer. The way to receive an answer is to sit quietly, relax, and then allow the mind to become as empty as possible waiting to see what comes. You will always receive an answer.

If a person can see his or her spirit guide or guardian - can that spirit see onto the physical plane too?

Of course, but it's as much a sensing as an envisioning.

Say I had a lucid dream and travelled somewhere in the physical with a spirit guide to a city such as New York - would that spirit see the city as well, and be able to communicate?

Yes, if you so choose.

Does a spirit guide actually appear onto this dimension or do we see that entity within its own realm?

It is your eyes in the physical dimension which create the forms of your beliefs. Although a spirit appears to be created by its arrival within your dimension, by the very fact of its being, it would be necessary for it to have originated on a spiritual plane.

Are these beings seen by our physical eyes or by a non-physical part of us?

They will appear to be real to your physical vision, for this is a natural manifestation of this energy. Therefore, even though you can see the spirit, more often than not, others can't.

Would a person communicating in words with a spirit in one's native language, hear the words inside of the mind?

Of course, they will only respond by using an individual's own language. It is important to bring into your awareness the fact that spirit guides are there to guide you. They would be of no help if people were unable to understand the communication.

Would the voice of the spirit be heard inside the mind and not externally?

Not necessarily, it would depend on a person's understanding. An image or a vision might be given instead. Sometimes, it's through the physical senses but on other occasions it's an internal feeling which can be called a gut feeling. There are many different ways in which these guides will communicate. To expect to have an on-going, highly lucid communication with a guide is not their purpose. These spirits are not there to tell you what to do but instead, to point out what it is you are doing.

Spirits are around you at all times. It's a matter of sensing them and being able to focus and channel them as well. This is what you would refer to as the astral planes utilizing your own terms. The way anyone sees them is a matter of how one connects to these energies.

I have a question about Doris Stokes, the famous English medium. She used to hear her spirit guide in her left ear. Any comments?

This is how she communicated.

Was it an actual voice that she heard? Did they make that pact before she came to earth?

Her primary means of communicating had more to do with hearing rather than seeing or speaking. This was the most convenient method. As to the pact, not necessarily, as all choices are open to an individual when entering onto the physical plane. The choices made during one's life will begin a directive towards certain outcomes which are things that an individual would wish to have happen or like to do. This allows each being to move towards different goals in each lifetime, rather than anticipating events because a lifetime has been preset and predetermined with contracts signed for a suggested outcome. It does not happen in this way.

When you talk about divine intervention, are you referring to the assistance of one's spiritual guides and the higher self as well?

In one sense yes, but some people misinterpret guides, thinking that they are a collection of superheroes waiting in the wings to save them. Guides are neither superheroes nor are they waiting to save you, and neither is some separate universal force. All individuals have received their own part of the universal mind. It's up to each entity to develop this, and by doing so, come into contact with those energies that we have been presenting to you. It's a matter of becoming sophisticated enough to interact on many different levels. It's being able to have the right thoughts and to make the correct choices when you undergo any state which is reactive. Each one of you must begin to direct those energies of which you are all a part.

When people see their guides or angels - what is happening in these situations?

Sometimes, you will observe the swirling of the life energy. This is what angels truly are - a combination of spirit and physical energy. Some of the more sensitive types see things more clearly than others. They might observe the true energy of a non-physical, rather than an angel in a white gown with fluffy wings or little pixies and fairies darting about.

What are spirit guides? Are these guides with us all of our lives and do they pass on messages, provide guidance in the sleep state, and perform other functions?

First, do not confuse angels with sprit guides. There is a difference. A spirit guide is the energy of an entity which had previously existed on the earth plane. It is one who chooses that role, is a member of the same soul group, and is part of a creative process with another soul who is physical. As a result, one entity is physical, and the soul aspect of the other can be viewed as representing a guide. Do understand that a guide is there to provide for feelings of security and furnish an understanding that one is not alone. Regarding the function of a guide to provide specific information or actually to do things for another soul, it's not a part of the process in the way that some imagine it to be.

There are those who would say that they have no wish to have somebody whispering in their ear and telling them what to do or what to think. The connection with a spirit guide does not exist in that way. The relationship tends to be one of providing insight, particularly the knowledge that the conscious mind has a link to the spirit realm which takes place through its connection with a spirit guide. These guides do exist and can be seen. To deal with certain conditions, it's possible to create an internal dialogue between a guide and oneself but most people don't experience this form of direct communication. Instead, they have a feeling of being protected and supported or a sense of having someone close or nearby. This allows an individual to feel comfortable, centred, and unafraid.

What occurs when people pray to God? Do the guides intervene?

Understand that every entity who would pray to God is also a part of that original creative energy. This is the only way it can be. Everyone is hooked into, or mainstreamed within that energy. So it is a part of you as you are a part it. You could not exist without that energy nor could that energy exist without you. It's a perfect symbiotic relationship. It's important to recognise that when someone's words are spoken to God, answers are not always revealed in the form of a burning bush. Alternatively, not always does a hand descend from heaven to pull someone out of trouble or difficulty.

Answers will appear in the form of other creations. Your prayers can be answered by those around you, or by circumstances which emerge as a result of your petitions. Intervention can come as a heightened sense of understanding about a situation which raises you above the pettiness of the interactions which were occurring at the time. By doing so, it will provide you will an opportunity to achieve more success, first as an individual and then in a biological and a reproductive sense as an integral member of your species.

When people have a problem or are dealing with a difficult situation - can they ask for guidance in the dream state? Is it possible to request that solutions be available to the conscious mind on awakening or that answers come into the mind sometime after the sleep period?

Of course, this is all a part of the channelling process. Any contact with a spirit guide is channelled information.

Concerning issues of free will and choice, I understand that the guides do not interfere directly. Do they sometimes prompt us to make certain decisions or to go in a particular direction, especially if we are to experience certain things during this life?

Be aware that all existence on your plane is a matter of free will, but free will does not mean being disconnected and deciding to do whatever it is that you want and then damn the consequences. Free will can involve consultation and determination of a path, as well as a plan of action. There might be many sources involved in any of your deliberations. By having an internal conversation such as the one we have described, this would be of benefit to any individual who has established those particular pathways of communication.

A psychic might see a spirit as a form of white or coloured light. How would that spirit see the psychic who is observing it? Would the spirit see another light or the physical representation of the psychic?

That non-physical being would see your energy or your spirit as you might call it. If there is a bonding between two entities, the non-physical being would be aware of a loop of energy connecting the two. There is no separation of consciousness just because one has a physical existence and the other does not.

To someone who is not clairvoyant - how would that person be aware of spirits?

Although some people believe themselves to be highly visual, this is not how they truly operate. Many function on an emotional level first, and then on what we will call a digital level which is an analytical mode that they fall into automatically. It's as if they turn on their personal computers. They attempt to determine what has been felt by distinguishing it intellectually to determine if it falls in line with what is being observed. All of it happens in less than a millisecond. So ofttimes, people can assume that they are highly visual, and yet, it's not their primary mode of functioning which is more on an intuitive or a feeling level.

Many people experience difficulty with the idea of seeing things which others do not. In one way, it might freak them out if suddenly, they saw lights and energies floating all about them. They might think that they had gone mad. Therefore, the emotional approach is a safer way. If someone does choose to see spirits, it can be done from within, through an internal visual representation of non-physical energies. Levels of comfort are up to each individual. For many, the emotional sensing is definitely the vehicle of choice.

Is there a way to communicate with the spirit guides that people actually see, even if they take the form of energies or colours?

What is important is your emotional responses, first of all to their colours, and then to the degree in which you are creating that feeling within you, the intensity so to speak. The communication which is coming through to you from these energies, as you observe them, comes through to you as an emotional response. Therefore, you must carefully listen to your emotional responses towards those actions and activities that you are seeing.

Is it a real event when angels appear to people and communicate? Can the voice of the angel really be heard in one's mind and are spirits able to communicate in this manner?

Yes.

So it would be a realistic communication.

Not only with an angel but any spirit. It's important to know that because an entity is not in the physical, it doesn't mean that such a being is not sentient or aware. How a non-physical represents itself to someone on the physical plane involves many factors. It will always appear in a manner in which a person feels comfortable, despite what people have said about having spirits appear to them in frightening guises.

How can someone open up an inner dialogue with one's guides? How can it be experienced as something which is real and not imaginary?

Each person has several or multiple guides and not just one. Some are there for a short time and then move on, while others are more permanent. Here is another concept related to spirit guides: Don't exclude those around you in the physical, for they are spirits too. You are a spirit and so are they. Some of your friends or relations can serve as spirit guides even though they are still in the flesh. They have information to impart to you through their own experience and their concern for your well-being. These are spirit guides too, and they can be included as contributors to your growth process as well.

Now, returning to the question of how to communicate with a guide who is non-corporeal. To achieve this, sit quietly and allow your mind to come to rest. Those of you, who are familiar with meditative techniques, select a procedure which provides you with both comfort and relaxation. For those who are not aware of how to meditate, it's a simple matter of sitting quietly in a darkened room. You can allow a small amount of light to emanate from behind your field of vision and play quiet music in the background. Preferably, the music should be classical with Mozart being the composer of choice, particularly any of his violin concertos. This will help to relax the mind and to create the conditions to move into a deeper state of relaxation.

We emphasise that the relaxation is to occur in your body and not your mind. It will be the mind which is the key to this process. We recommend that you record the following information which will allow you to enter into an altered state. Once you have become relaxed, your recording will provide the following instructions:

You are now in a deep state of relaxation. As you notice how relaxed your body is, be aware of how sharp your mind has become. By using the keenness of your mind, recall a time when you were somewhere which was very comfortable and very secure. As you feel this warmth all about you, know that this was a place where you were held in very high esteem. Allow yourself to drift back and return to that moment.

That special time could have been a gathering of your family or a time when you were being honoured, or perhaps it was with friends when you were being appreciated for something that you did or said. No matter what event you have chosen, simply return to that time. Allow yourself to feel that wonderful feeling of self as you are completely at one with your own consciousness.

As you are in this place become aware of another presence. This presence feels like an old friend, a person with whom you have always felt a great comfort and joy whenever you were together. Feel this friendly presence in your special place, but just off to one side and behind your right shoulder. Notice that even though this person is behind you, there is a feeling of comfort and relaxation. Allow that feeling to enter into your heart, body and mind. As you do this, we recommend that you simply take a moment and in your mind, shift your focus towards your right shoulder; you can slowly open your inner eyes for a moment if you wish.

As you do this, you will see or sense a shadow which has always seemed to be there. As it begins to move out in front of you, follow it until you are once again facing forward. Notice that it is a person, and as you observe, note that the individual is not facing you. Allow this person to turn around and look right at you. Take a moment to look at the face, and pay attention to any special details. Is it male or female? Is this entity a human? No matter what, take a moment to observe what you are seeing. Allow all of it to enter your consciousness. Notice that whatever or whomever this individual is, that a feeling of love, understanding, and a complete unity is projected to you from that figure.

This is your spirit guide. Your guide has been made manifest in this special place. As you look at the spirit guide, become aware of the wisdom, the love, and the willingness of this entity to share and provide knowledge. Take a moment and ask a question about something to which you need an immediate answer. Once you have asked the question, wait for the response.

The answer might not come to you in words. It can arrive through a vision, a picture or feeling, but it will manifest within you. Whether it's through a visual, auditory or emotional means, this is how your spirit guide communicates. Whichever one is appropriate for you, accept it into your heart. Listen for the information, feel for it, and absorb it into your very self. As you do this, you will find that whatever you need to know is being answered in a direct manner. Perhaps it might be something which does not appear to make sense or seem appropriate. The answer might not always be something that you consider fits your question, or a response that you feel is correct.

You can enter into a dialogue with this guide and ask a number of questions. You can request the entity's name, origins, and the reason for your particular connection. Just as important, you can enquire about your own mission in life and the truths of existence.

When you have completed your dialogue by asking these questions and any others that you might have, realise that you may return to this place anytime you wish. You can rejoin this spirit guide and continue to carry on these exchanges which have occurred.

Now it's time to say goodbye. Before you do, look at the spirit guide and send your love, appreciation, and your thanks for all which has been revealed to you. As you do so, notice that your guide reaches inside to a hidden place and removes a small object. It's a special gift. Hold out your hand and receive your gift as it is presented to you. Do not look at it directly, but cup your hands around it and thank your spirit guide by sending love from your heart. Realize that everything will continue to be at your beck and call whenever you return to this timeless time, and this placeless place that you have now entered.

As the spirit guide fades and you feel more and more centred, you are returning to your normal state of consciousness. With your inner vision, take a moment to open your hands and to look at the gift that the spirit guide has left. As you are looking, ask yourself about this gift and see if you are able to determine what it is.

Observe it from all angles. Feel its weight and notice the colours. Observe the energy running through it. Perceive it in any way that you can. Realise what that gift means in relation to your own life and growth. Truly, what you have received is a gift of the mind. It's a gift to help raise your understanding and your level of consciousness. Once you have understood that gift, and you have communicated with it in a way which allows you to grasp all of the truths which are held within it, slip the gift away. Store it in that special place where all such gifts are kept, and once again, thank your guide even though you can no longer see that spirit.

Bring yourself back into the present by counting from one to ten. With each ascending number, you will find yourself becoming more and more established within the physical world. Your communication with your spirit guide will begin to become integrated within you on all levels of consciousness: the physical, emotional, mental and spiritual.

When this communication has become fully integrated and you have comprehended it totally, slowly open your eyes. From now on, you will be able to go forward in your life and take this information with you.

During this activity, should one's physical eyes always be closed?

This activity is to be internalised. Within the theatre of the mind, there must be the awareness of the eyes opening and closing within the experience itself. Inside, the eyes are open. The entity experiencing the process will be exploring from within. It's a visual contemplation from inside oneself. Opening and closing the eyes remains an internal process. You are looking with the inner eye. The physical eyes do not open until the final countdown and your return to physical reality.

What we have provided is a method by which you might attempt to meet your spirit guide on an internal basis. You may want to record this technique or alternatively, read through it and then practice it after committing it to memory. Another approach is to have someone whom you trust read it to you, but only after that individual has become familiar with the correct pauses, and the timing of each step in the process. If you practice this technique, it will begin to provide you with a true communication with your spirit guides.

- 5 -

EXTRATERRESTRIALS

I am wondering about extraterrestrials and other forms of consciousness within the physical universe. How does non-terrestrial life compare to human consciousness?

First of all, it is important to consider the consciousness of humanity. Generally speaking, humankind suffers from an inferiority complex. This arises from the understanding that humans are mortal. No matter how brilliant, no matter how clever, no matter how witty, no matter how dominant, no matter how anything human that you are, you are also mortal. There is a beginning and an end.

This arises from humanity viewing itself solely as physical matter linked to the earth. Saying point blank to someone that there is a God, is no different than saying to a dog that there is a cat. It doesn't mean anything until interactivity occurs. Such interaction is only possible through an internal experience of feeling on an emotional level. This is taking an intellectual aspect and turning it into an emotional reality. Once understood on an emotional basis, then there is an opportunity for taking the next step towards an understanding of the truth of mortality versus immortality.

Now, extending this analogy to the consideration of extraterrestrials, there exists the idea that aliens are superior, both intellectually and emotionally. This is not necessarily true. The reason that humanity considers extraterrestrials to be superior, is due to the fact that mankind continues to remain earthbound, relatively speaking. Whilst there are small rockets which move away from the earth, there are also radiations out there which literally fry entities who attempt to go too far off-planet.

If we introduce concepts such as interdimensionality or the ability to move between dimensions, these terms are almost impossible for the average human being to grasp on any level, unless it's within the realms of science fiction. It's an irony that by introducing it as science fiction, this is how things are accepted and believed. There is a growing understanding that aliens are now a part of your culture, whether they are physically here, such as the Harpies during the times of Ulysses, or in modern times in the form of the Greys.

Such writings have emerged through mythology, and in fact, there is already a belief which has emerged which considers all of this as myth. At this time, there are many ideas concerning extraterrestrials. Arguments are irrelevant for as you know, these entities are not only real, but are integrated into the human and social spheres on your planet. As well, they have taken part in the development of your technology.

Can you comment on the controversy surrounding abductions?

If it were necessary to abduct - what would be the point? If these aliens are already operating within your societies, then abductions are no different than your bogeyman phenomena. There are those who believe that abduction has happened to them. There is a similarity amongst the stories told by those who have provided information about lost time. There are numerous other likenesses as well. Yes, these abductions do occur and have taken place. It happens mostly to individuals who have been tracked throughout their lives, much the same as scientists chart the movements of a dolphin or a rare bird.

When you mention off-planet, I imagine that you are talking about extraterrestrials. Are there some groups which have an interest in interfering here while others have a desire to let things be and to assist?

Yes.

Are some of these extraterrestrials participating in our societies at present?

Yes, but what you do not appreciate - as it's only hinted at during these times - is that all human beings who exist on your planet share a common extraterrestrial origin. As a result, you can include yourselves amongst them. Extraterrestrial influence has already come onto this plane. The richness of your existence did not originate solely within your corner of the universe; it has been spread in other ways in past times. It's untrue that there are those who are attempting to connect and interrelate with human beings for the purpose of domination. There are other ulterior motives involved, but mostly, entities whose origins are from outside of your earth are curious about you.

In the past, those whose intentions were to interfere with humans desired to control the planet. By dominating your world, it would provide more space for their species. As well, some held an original belief that there could be connectivity to the earth through a form of hybridization which would allow them to migrate onto the earth. In reality, they were unable to exist upon your planet due to the atmospheric conditions. Those whom you refer to as the Greys, have left your world and are no longer here. They are of another base and what you are seeing in popular fiction and urban myths, are simply reflections of the energy form that these entities truly represent.

The Greys interconnect by affiliating with the physical plane. The Greys have taken that which is contained within themselves and within all entities - the energy of inner exploration - and attempted to reproduce it outside of themselves or externally. These entities possess an ability to sit together and create an energy mind. This allows them to move about as a collective consciousness into other dimensions, and into other places and spaces.

Such innate abilities to move about in this manner are no longer valued by these entities. They have externalized these inner aspects through the use of technology, and therefore, replaced their inner capabilities with technology. Again, this is not a conspiracy, it is simply their own predilection and direction, and it must be understood that this is a part of their learning within their own particular existence.

So what can you do about these extraterrestrials? Observe and watch, but you don't have to remain helpless. Simply regard these interconnections with off-planet beings as fascinating, but how to become part and parcel of this alien drama is a question that many will ask themselves: *How do I get involved? Should I get involved? Is there any purpose in getting involved?* Prior to any of these considerations, there must be an understanding of one's individual consciousness including a comprehension of one's relationship to existence itself.

Regarding extraterrestrials, there was a book released by a retired Lt. Colonel of the United States military about the Roswell crash. Although this book has been challenged as to its accuracy, the author talks about the creation of the Star Wars program which was an attempt to dissuade certain extraterrestrial groups from interfering with the earth because they had been buzzing our spacecraft. Are there any truths to these statements?

Yes, but the Star Wars program was geared towards aiming out from the earth, and not onto the earth. There was a misunderstanding that Russia and the United States were rushing to create this amazing technology for espionage and warfare. In fact, there was a cooperative network which existed during those times to create a relationship of protective measures to prevent invasions of the earth.

Recently you mentioned our space brothers. Are extraterrestrials going to become involved in our earth changes by assisting mankind or will they stand back and observe? Are they involved now?

There are several layers of involvement. Primarily, for the moment, it's observation. Be aware that there are some who have entered onto your planet already, becoming active within the political scene and other scenarios currently underway. Consequently, it becomes a process of intertwining the energies of your planet with those from another. These off-planet entities are involved in making decisions as well. In fact, they have made agreements with some upon the earth to provide certain technological information which would allow the western alliance to move forward.

Would this be part of Area 51 in Nevada and the United States secret military operations?

Yes, and this is where some of the experiments with the technology are being carried out. You must consider also, the areas of Montauk, Long Island, as well as regions of the Nevada and New Mexico deserts. These developments have not been based on alien technology which has been taken from downed spaceships, but technology which has been shared with you by off-planet civilisations.

You have mentioned that there are at least twelve different extraterrestrial civilisations which interact with the earth. Do they belong to some form of intergalactic association?

There are far more than twelve but there are twelve major alliances here at this time. It's not important for you to have their names, as it would be irrelevant. Needless to say, we will tell you that there are those who hold different types of energies and originate from other planets. Yes, there are the White Giants and those whom you refer to as the Greys and the Blues.

Extraterrestrials come from many different backgrounds. Some are reptilianlike, while others hold forms similar to your insects. There are many who exhibit a humanoid form in one manner or another. It's an automatic understanding amongst these groups that if different species choose to interact with one another, especially on a technological basis, then all will have the greatest chance for survival. This is why the earth has been contacted in the past and also accounts for the sharing of technology at this time. There is no great prime directive as some of you have been led to believe through Star Trek and programs of that ilk. The only prime directive is that life should persevere through its own process, and that existence in a sentient form should continue within an infinite universe of mystery.

Do these alien groups have far more spiritual knowledge than humans?

Not necessarily, but there is certain information that many extraterrestrials have a great interest in, particularly the human psyche. There is a curiosity about your ability to love and to show feelings of love, and the fact that love goes beyond an act of procreation and extends into the more esoteric areas or what you understand to be spiritual growth. It's most important to these entities to study such matters and their resultant behaviours because the human experience is so foreign to their own ways of being.

What has occurred for many who visit your planet - those who hold alien perspectives - is that they have lost their capacity to emotionally express in many areas. The reason is that other aspects of their brains have been developed, allowing brain activity which would normally be taken up with emotional activity to become involved with cerebral functioning and intellectual performance. This permits a far greater ability to produce results pertaining to the intellect.

All eyes are upon the earth at this time. Although many of the connections are on a spiritual level, let's return to your question about these entities being more spiritually advanced. In many instances this is not the case. In some circumstances, they have such an advanced understanding of technology that if it were to be shared, it would raise the level of consciousness for many on your planet.

Is the President of the United States aware of alien involvement at Area 51, or is it kept secret from Washington?

The President is aware of it.

Humans communicate with each other mainly through a spoken or verbal language. How do extraterrestrials communicate with one another? Is it done telepathically or is there a universal language?

Those who work together from different parts of the universe are more concerned with their own outcomes rather than what happens to others who share the universe with them. Regarding a universal language, all types of communication are used. At this time, most are looking out for their own interests. There are few which have the magnanimous understanding of the importance of interconnecting with other intelligent species.

Is it possible for someone to meet with an alien consciousness? Can anyone selectively choose such an event?

No, not in the manner that you are suggesting. It's not like calling on your favourite Uncle Martin. There's a juncture where extraterrestrials do communicate and often, that connection is through the pineal. It's important to note that the correct nutrition for the pineal is a dedication to meditation and a singleness of mind. This will help you to raise your consciousness beyond the veil so to speak, and to enter into a higher state of consciousness. In an altered state of communication, interaction is possible with other entities on all levels of life and in other planetary locations.

So communication on another level is possible in an altered state of consciousness.

Yes, in that type of meditative state, you will have an opportunity to communicate with alien intelligence. Be aware that these entities are not really alien to you. All entities upon the earth have previously existed elsewhere in past lives, and have not necessarily returned only to the earth. People have lived in numerous extraterrestrial environments themselves, and as a result possess an underlying understanding of these energies.

Can you provide us with a physical description of a being from Sirius?

They are similar to dolphins. Do understand that dolphins did not arrive on your planet in the manner that you might imagine. There are vast distances between planetary and star systems. In your measurements, this amounts to several light years. These entities had mastered the art of shifting from planet to planet and system to system by means of a thought vehicle. Such movement can be considered similar to a physical creation, and in a manner of speaking, also construed to be of a physical nature, but in truth, such motion is engendered by, powered by, and operated by, either one individual consciousness or that of several, in combination.

What this proves is that thought can move faster than light. As soon as a thought about a particular thing is projected, then that object has a direct connection to the thought, which in turn, can be traced back to its originator or that which produced it in the first place. So indeed, thinking is the best way to travel. This is how the beings from Sirius came to your planet, travelling in this manner.

Even though they arrive as a mental creation, they still have an effect on the physical environment surrounding them, thus enabling them to connect with both land and sea creatures. They connected first with the inhabitants of the sea who possessed a similar physiology, and interestingly, a parallel psychology as well.

What is their physical form on their own planet of Sirius?

They are an aquatic species with similarities to a dolphin.

How do they survive?

These beings are very efficient, and have adapted well to their environment, living for an extended length of time and not bothered by any natural predators. They are virtually of pure mind because of the existence they hold. They can move outside of their physical confines, and not only between physical worlds, but amongst spiritual dimensions as well. These entities possess a greater mobility than you can ever imagine.

On your plane, never forget that there exists a natural propensity for all beings to evolve to a point of reconnecting with their spiritual origins. When one circle is complete then the next stage of growth will emerge.

Are the beings from Sirius similar to us in a spiritual manner? Do they have a soul which has taken a different form to ours for its physical existence?

Ask yourself this question. Many of you hold within yourselves other lifetimes in this system.

You have mentioned this previously. Would the method for tracing such origins be self-exploratory?

If you so desire. The best way for you to accomplish this is to ensure that from time to time, you make it to open water. Take the opportunity not just to swim with the dolphins, but to catch sight of them and to be in their company. As this takes place, you will feel your connection. Simply open your mind and allow it to be a conduit for the images, impulses and energies, that dolphins naturally send your way.

I love to visit dolphin aquariums. I just love to be around them.

Yes, but there's sadness in those places - is there not?

Yes, and that's why I asked that original question, because it always bothers me to see them in those small tanks, and to watch them performing for humanity. I enjoy visiting the dolphins in order to be around them, but I always feel that they should be out in the ocean and free.

This is one of their ways of communicating. Some of them have sacrificed themselves to be available for humans. When they perform, dolphins do not consider themselves to be buffoons. They are demonstrating to humans that even in confinement, they will continue to hold grace and beauty, and therefore, they serve as an exhibit of how to elevate everyday consciousness above the mundane. For themselves, dolphins can do this on a daily basis.

When you wonder about captivity being either good or bad, the answer is that it's not good to confine any creature. Until the consciousness of humanity moves beyond the need to treat all other creatures as inferior, this is the only way in which dolphins can communicate and maintain their integrity with human beings, while simultaneously, projecting this awareness into the consciousness of mankind.

You have said that these dolphins are very intelligent creatures, and that they are connected to life forms within the planetary system of Sirius.

Do dolphins mind travel as well? Are they able to move away from their physical bodies contained within the holding tanks?

Yes, when they choose to do so. They do not have the same lines or distinctions between the conscious and unconscious as humans do, where in one state you are awake, and in the other you are sleeping or dreaming. It's a matter of choice as they are not confined only to the physical body.

You mentioned that the beings from Sirius travelled by a thought vehicle. Were you referring to thought as the vehicle?

We will explain it in this way. When thought is amalgamated, and in particular, combined with several other thought forms, an energy vehicle can be created. From this, images can be transferred to others in different locals. UFO's are an example. When such a thought vehicle is created, travel is instantaneous.

Certainly not all extraterrestrials travel in this manner. Do some have actual physical vehicles? There are stories about extraterrestrial spacecraft crashing onto the earth, and that these vehicles were thought driven.

There are certain lines of energy which are universal. They are more concentrated in some areas than in others. These lines of energy have been studied by others within the physical universe, and it was discovered that by exciting these lines, that in fact, instantaneous movement could take place along their trajectories. You can refer to them as magnetic lines which are part of a universal gridlock or pattern. Even though you cannot actually see this phenomenon, all of the stars and all of the objects in the universe are connected by lines of energy of this nature. This process allows them to remain equidistant over great epochs of time. These are utilised in a physical sense by what you think of as a space vehicle which moves along such lines. In reality, many things are very different from what your entertainment industry has indicated through science fiction over the years.

The way in which we treat dolphins, such as keeping them in small holding tanks - do they accept this because it keeps them connected to mankind? I feel that this is something which should not be happening.

Yes, it's something which should not be done. It's the same as if you are imprisoning them. What if you jailed a human being and then exposed that person to dolphins only? What if that person was allowed only an occasional visit from another human, but the visitor had been raised solely around dolphins as well, and so the only reference would be dolphins. Such unnatural conditions would create abnormal behaviour.

With dolphins, they are far more effective when existing in the oceans with their own kind. Realize that dolphins held in tanks, have a mental connection with other dolphins elsewhere on your planet. There is a certain degree of dolphin consciousness that we'll refer to as the collective unconscious for dolphins. This network allows them to tie into each other much more effectively than any human can. Dolphin consciousness has evolved to the point where they realise that it is not the sound that they make which is communicated, but the thoughts they send. This is how dolphins find humans in the middle of the ocean and attempt to save them.

When humans are around dolphins, the energy that they give off makes us feel very happy. In particular, dolphin energy affects our emotions. What happens?

Dolphins are connected to influences outside of, and beyond your planet. Dolphins are a part of a cosmic consciousness. They are bound to the universe, just as all of you are linked, but they are also wedded to their progenitors and to those who truly support their existence in the water. As we have stated, dolphins are linked to Sirius.

When humans associate with dolphin energy, there is a sense of homecoming. It's a sense of connectivity to other creatures which hold similar understandings of life as you. At all times, dolphins exude a sense of freedom and movement. It's a sense of totally living and experiencing their purpose by simply existing. They live a pure, clean and clear existence, and this is easily recognizable to all.

The crash of an alien spaceship at Roswell in 1947 was a physical occurrence. Does the United States still possess that vehicle?

Of course, and they are in possession of many other vehicles of this nature. The bodies were recovered as well. These craft are scouting ships, and not star ships which move from galaxy to galaxy. There are numerous entities in many parts of the universe, using and applying different forms of energy. They connect with each other by various means, depending on the evolutionary stage of each species involved.

You have spoken about communicating with extraterrestrials by expanding one's consciousness. Would you provide us with a very simple method for connecting?

Hold your index finger horizontally, with the tip about six inches away from the nose. The finger should be gradually moved upward by several inches as the eyes follow. This creates a trigger mechanism for the release of certain endorphins within the brain. It creates a feeling of well-being and expanded consciousness. As the mind opens, it will facilitate new concepts much more easily.

Are you suggesting that this process will take one away from conditioned responses, and redirect one's attention to things outside of the self? Does this altered focus allow for a different type of perception?

Haven't you discovered this already?

Can you talk more about extraterrestrial involvement with the earth?

They are involved. Your expanding technology has been a result of this from the beginning. It has been affected by the overall physiological connection to aliens, as you call them. Realise that wherever there is mass or the planetoid collective material of creation in the universe, there is an identical opportunity for the creation of life. This is due to the physicality of how life works on the physical plane. There must be something for spirit to enter into in order to become self-aware, and that's the important aspect of physicality. So there exists the spontaneous creation of life in all parts of the universe, which in turn, will begin to move towards a central matrix for the express purpose of reconnecting with itself on a conscious level. It's a natural coming together of all life forms.

So it's important that all sentient life interacts with itself, and then it can either destroy itself, or work towards a compensatory relationship to share what is possessed or to provide what is lacking. Your earth societies have reached this point before, on many occasions. It's a process of fermentation. Humankind is now in the position where its consciousness is beginning to link more completely. This is due to the high energy levels on the earth at this time. It's also the result of the constant waves of civilisations which have come and gone on your planet, ebbing and flowing, and creating generation after generation, civilisation after civilisation.

This can be compared to the creation a Samurai sword. It's not only a product of heating metal and then pounding it into shape. There is a continual folding, flattening, shaping and heating on a repeated basis. It is melded continuously, which changes the fabric of the actual sword. Through the different expressions of the metal by this repetitive process, eventually, a metal blade of great strength and beauty is created. If examined under an electron microscope, one would observe that the actual structure of the atoms was strengthened as a result of the manufacturing procedures of flattening and folding.

The same holds true for society and humankind, which has fermented to the point where it can now be decanted and made ready for its interaction with the universal vintage. Our metaphor is used to indicate the same consistent growth which takes place in your wine industry and creates better and better vintages by continuing to use more advanced techniques.

It's the same with societies. The societies on your planet as they exist today have an enormous potential to make this connection on a global basis. This is despite the dissension in various parts of the world. There is a worldwide movement for human consciousness to awaken to its own original source. In the past, as covenants were broken, so was the social wholeness of society. It has taken many generations since then, to reach the point of a golden age, whereby, the countries and people of the world have now gone beyond a flashpoint. By the very nature of creation, the next stage must be a movement towards a new vision regarding the wholeness of humanity. Although this unification will begin slowly and occur mainly through political means, eventually, society will become consolidated once again and enter into a new world social order.

At this moment, what is occurring through the world's monetary coalitions represents a part of this process in the form of a worldwide desire to pull together. Humanity is not meant to be drawn together just by a privileged few, although this is what is taking place at present. This impetus which is considered by many to be negative or evil has passed beyond the control of those who think they are in charge, and as a result, they can only provide a very limited direction.

I have a question about the accuracy of particular descriptions of extraterrestrials. Any comments?

It's important for you to realise that in a universe of infinite probabilities, all things are possible. Therefore, the descriptions which have been depicted are reflective of some of those species. It is important to note that all of these entities have developed towards the form of a single head and body, as well as two arms and legs. This includes a digital grasp and a circulatory system to carry energies about the body. You can begin to see how similar life is wherever you go. Despite the differences in size, which depends upon physiology and the origins of one's planet, there is a sameness of coordination among various species when a certain degree of understanding has been reached.

I have a question about ET activity. We talked about them arriving by means of a tear in the space-time fabric, and that they actually do come here. You have mentioned that they experience difficulty with our radiation.

They don't have difficulty with the radiation, but with the atmosphere. They do not breathe in the same ratio as you do. They have much higher metabolic requirements for oxygen. They feel the same as you do when you are breathing in water.

I saw a program about a live alien who was supposedly filmed in a military establishment in the U. S. It appeared to be a smallish figure who was dying. No one has been able to establish whether or not this film is fictional. Are you able to locate this incident and comment?

Here's the story. This was a reconstruction of something which truly did happen. It was through the wishes of those who created it, to allow others to have a vision of what in fact, had occurred.

There is another film, in which doctors are operating on some small bodies, supposedly, after the Roswell crash. Is this a fiction as well?

Yes, it's fictitious.

You have stated that the Roswell crash did occur, and that bodies were recovered as well as the spaceship.

Yes.

Are those small spaceships driven by a pilot with an electronic headband, creating a unit which allows that entity to become a part of the craft? Was that small ship from a mother craft?

Yes, to both questions. These would be the Greys.

Are they are okay once inside the craft where their atmosphere is stable according to their needs?

Yes.

When the Roswell ship crashed, some were killed instantly while the remaining ones died shortly thereafter - was it because of the atmosphere and not being able to breathe?

To a degree. There was one survivor taken into captivity. It communicated telepathically with those humans surrounding it, which was very disconcerting for them. It was important for the Roswell event to occur, because it began to create the knowledge that the next step in human evolution was not going to be physiological but psychospriritual, which is the ability to communicate outside of physical means.

There were six involved in the crash. One of the aliens who was taken, lived until your year of 1951, when it died. It was part of an experiment conducted by the government. It was President Truman who authorised it, and he maintained the situation until the year before he left office. Many experiments have been conducted which have provided some of the technology which is currently in use.

When the alien spoke telepathically - was it in English?

It was thought projection. Not thoughts in the way that you would understand them, but in the form of images.

Can any aliens communicate in English telepathically? Can they send words into someone else's head?

No, it's different. It's as if one hears thoughts inside the head. It's different.

So, it's a thought in which you know what the other person's meaning is, but you don't actually hear the words.

Yes, and it works more on an emotional level which is how thinking is. When contact takes place mind to mind, it's important to know that during this type of communication, there is an emotional response which occurs,. The difficulties that aliens experience in connecting with human beings, is that your emotions are still raw, and not as well-defined or finely developed as those of the aliens.

Therefore, it's painful for them to communicate with you as a species. There have been other connections which have occurred over the years, and not just with the United States government. Extraterrestrials have been involved with certain monetary interests and banking concerns behind the world governments.

The ideas surrounding conspiracy, as have been perpetrated by your media and entertainment vehicles such as the X-Files, are only partially true. This acts as a smokescreen to prevent people from seeing the larger picture. In one sense, at this time, the earth is on trial within the intergalactic community. There are only a few on the earth who are aware of this situation. The growth and development of those on the earth is being observed, and it will continue to be, to determine when humankind is ready to achieve the next stage of growth.

There is a breakthrough occurring at this very moment. Your levels of awareness, consciousness, and ultimately, the sophistication of your mental processes, are in their incipient stages. There are many who have reached beyond this point, and many others who are on the verge of conversion. It has nothing to do with physicality, but only perception, and how you perceive that which occurs about you. This is the difference. When this change takes place, then a connection with the alien races will happen.

Can you provide a time frame for that to occur?

You are quite close at present. That is the reason for the strong input from extraterrestrials at this time. In years gone by, this type of subject would have been treated with extreme disdain. Now, these topics receive a certain amount of respect and concern. This allows those on the earth an opportunity to have this connection with alien intelligence on their televisions, in movie theatres, and appearing within popular fiction.

It's part of a larger program, to begin acclimatizing your world towards that ultimate contact, but it is not being made very public at this time.

With the Greys, it is my understanding that they have externalized their emotions, and are unable to feel like we do. Is this correct?

Yes, this is why emotional contact through mental telepathy is difficult for them.

Are they attempting to re-establish their emotions once again?

No, and they are neither happy nor unhappy with the way they are. They are unemotional.

Are the Greys really doing experiments to create a hybrid race between themselves and humans?

This is fiction. It's already happened. What do you think you are?

You have already stated that what exists as humankind on the earth is a hybrid form of other alien races.

Yes.

So we are evolving into a more mature stage where humanity can take its place within the intergalactic community.

Yes, that's one way to view it, but it's not like you are standing in line. What is occurring on your planet at this time, is a particular growth which has been unprecedented in the annuls of intergalactic history. The leaps by humanity which are currently underway have never occurred in other developing life forms outside of your world.

There is so much interest at this time by outsiders, and hence, the upsurge in activity around your planet. Also, there are large numbers of extraterrestrial observers, either in residence or in direct proximity, surveying the incorporation of the human mind.

So when you observe the current wars on your planet, and consider those who have been branded as the "evil ones", it has to do with the outcropping of this growth process. As your species continues in its evolution, it will have the opportunity to move into new standards of what will be considered to be positive traits for the human experience.

Are you referring to a world consciousness and unity, rather than to our current nationalistic identities? Mustn't we recognize ourselves as spiritual beings first and physical entities second?

Yes, it's important to see this, but don't forget the larger connection. The larger link is to a collective consciousness. We are speaking of collective consciousness rather than unconsciousness.

The collective consciousness is what is important, and it is now being wedged into the human experience. This will allow for all individuals on your planet to grow through these types of revelations.

You have mentioned that there is no direct connection with extraterrestrials now, but you have said that some of these groups are linked to old money interests who already know about ET's and have had contact. You made another statement that there is currently no contact because of the atmospheric conditions.

It's the Greys who have difficulty with the atmosphere. Contacts with certain interests on your planet, is one of extended contact, and one which does not necessarily necessitate the physical attendance of these extraterrestrials. What is also important to understand, is that with the intelligence and advances of these individual races, there is also the opportunity for transmogrification of individuals to create what you would call hybrids. There has been much written and fantasized about this, but the absolute truth is that there is no conscious desire by extraterrestrials to enslave, capture, or generally utilize your world for their own purposes and evil.

For indeed, you must understand that these energies, whether they be of pure intellect or a variation of such, all of them have a greater consciousness than those on the earth plane. As a result, as you would look upon chimpanzees as lovable little rascals which must be contained, in much the same way, these entities view those in your world in a similar light, just to give you an idea of their perspectives.

Therefore, there is no negativity attached to the larger picture, but what remains ingrained within humanity, is still based upon greed and self-aggrandisement. This is important to understand. Be aware that certain energies outside of your earth plane, have utilized these aspects of humanity to try to help the earth on a grander scale, choosing to back some of the activities of the stronger power groups of your world, so there can be a faster unification of the planet. So in this way, there have been interconnections.

With some of those contacts, are there any extraterrestrial groups which can exist within our atmosphere?

Yes.

So they breathe oxygen. Do some of them make their presence known?

Yes, they have done so in the past, as well as now. They are also doing it as walk-ins, to use your concepts and terminology. This is something which has to be comprehended from an interdimensional point of view, as well as understanding that it works on a spiritual level as well. Therefore, it crosses the fine line between aliens and spirit. For indeed, there are no true aliens, only advanced forms of consciousness which exist in slightly different physical formats.

The ideal format for physical movement is any similarity to the human form. Most of those entities you would consider to be humanoid, or alien, are all human in one sense or another. In this sense, there is a genetic connectivity amongst all. For they and you, are all linked to the same physical energies and rules of creation. So, many of the extraterrestrial energies or aliens, are similar in physical form and have needs akin to your own.

Currently, scientists are attempting to peer into other universes and galaxies to determine stars similar in size to your sun, or to identify systems which have a number of planets floating about them. All of it is being calculated by your finest computers, whose tallies have come up with numbers into the billions within the visible universe. It's understood that the universe is infinite, and what is picked up by your radio telescopes, is minuscule, or one nth of a degree of the totality of That Which Is.

Therefore, it's not just a matter of imagining worlds where there would be other humans, but also to understand the development of your world in the manner in which it has come about, including how intelligent life has arisen as the human species, or how it evolved as that creature you call modern man. At the same time, these connections to entities and energies from other planets are similar, even though there might be differentiation in the physical aspects. What is most important, is that intelligence has developed with a spiritual aspect to it in all of these entities, in all of these races, and in all of these creatures. Therefore, this is the connecting and divine aspect of aliens and humans, which are the higher aspects of consciousness and the soul.

All have soul. Therefore, the thought that there would be disconnection from these extraterrestrials is odd, particularly from those who are able to come to your earth as a result of their technology, and just as interesting, by means of their spiritual advances. So you see, those who arrive on your planet are not exactly what you would call intergalactic adventurers hoping to stake a claim upon the planet earth.

It's important for people to begin to realize the oneness of consciousness which exists within their own selves, because this will allow them to feel connected to all other forms of existence and intelligence. It will allow for an individual to feel more and more united on a larger and grander scale.

There has been a myth, a cult, and a culture building up around extraterrestrials, creating much fear upon your plane, particularly for those who are plugged into conspiracy theories or fears pertaining to intrigue and collusion. These are the ones who may indeed find validity in their fears, because they attempt to carry out their research in this way. The truth is, that the less an individual focuses and concentrates on these things, the greater the opportunity for people to discover their own spiritual centres, and to feel connected through feelings of love and unity, rather than feelings of separateness accompanied by fear and paranoia.

You have mentioned that first contact for the masses is not too far off, perhaps as little as thirty years away. How will it take place should such an event occur?

Through your normal release of information. When it is important for the general population to understand that there is a connection between the earth and outside forces and energies, then it will be released through your news media.

With first contact, people always imagine a space craft landing - how might it take place?

It will be a meeting between individuals, and broadcast to the world. Definitive differences in physiology will be shown.

What type of ET's? Will they be Greys, Blues?

They will be a humanoid form, with a skin colour close to yours, but yellowish with a blue undertone. They will have humanoid energies and be of a shorter stature. These would be Syrians.

You had mentioned before that the Syrians are dolphinlike as well. Would it be the same species?

Understand that this is how they would appear to humans.

In a humanoid form?

Yes.

But on their own planet they are a water species.

Originally, yes. The best way to describe what you will be seeing, is a mental projection which has gathered physical substance on you plane to create a physical representation. Understand that the next steps that you hold in your human development are mental and spiritual evolution. Individuals will have the ability to project their consciousness into other locales, and not only to project, but also, to gain substance, appear in different forms, and give different impressions to those who see them.

Can you give us a personal activity to help practice something like that?

Yes, it is simply this: First of all, begin to take your consciousness and move it about your body. You may realize that you have your concentration contained within your head, but not necessarily. We suggest that you sit quietly in a darkened room, with a dim light placed from behind. It is important to begin to ask yourself specifically: *Who is thinking?* When you begin to ask this question, as the thinking process occurs, note who is thinking and from where the thoughts are being generated. Once you realize this location in the body - and we mean in the body and not outside of it - pinpoint where these thoughts are generated or being received. Wherever this occurs in your body, that's the location of your mind.

Once you have a conceptual understanding of this process, you will then have the ability to consciously move your mind about the body. For example, if you discover that you mind is in your chest, then you can move it up into your head where you would perceive and conceive of your body through this locale. Next, you might move your consciousness into a hand or a fingertip and perceive your mind and concentration from that point.

Initially, do this for approximately one week, practising for ten to fifteen minutes per day. At the end of this time, if you have not mastered this ability, continue until you do. If you have, however, the next step is to project your mind around the room. Without moving from wherever you are, imagine seeing the room from the upper south-east corner. Allow your consciousness to flow to this locale, until you can truly see the room from this other perspective.

Once you are adept at this behaviour, which might take another week to three weeks, you can then shift to an outside location. If you have pets, begin to project yourself by seeing the world through their eyes. You are not moving into their consciousness, but into their view of the world. A good way to do this is to imagine the head of your pet as being larger than your own head as it looks in your direction. In meditation, you would then reach for that head, turn it around, and slip it over your own head. Next, begin to see the world through the eyes of the animal, including the how, what, when and where.

Once you have done this, you can experiment with other orientations, such as a bird, a tree or a rock, and begin to project your consciousness into other situations. You might think that it's your imagination, but as you know, it is imagination which is the basis for these abilities and all abilities for that matter. Once you have reached this certain point, begin to project yourself into areas that you are familiar with around the house. Experience them as if you were there, by seeing whatever you can see. The longer you are able to stay in another locale, the easier it becomes to observe what is in that actual place.

After you have practised this for another few weeks, eventually, you will find that you have the ability to say to yourself: *I would like to materialize here.* Allow you imagination to recreate your physical body in that place, but again, it's done by using the imagination. In truth, by this time, your projections should be slightly visible to those in the room. The first thing that they will sense is a presence, and as your practice continues, they will notice the appearance of your very self.

All told, depending on your capabilities, it might take one to two years to develop. What is crucial in this particular instance is consistency. The most important thing is to practice, practice, and practice.

Be aware that consciousness is not limited to physical conditions only. It's the projection of your awareness into the circumstances of wherever it's directed. In other words, if a consciousness desires to experience a certain form of existence, it can simply project itself into the same.

This is the potential that all of you hold within yourselves as human beings. Many on your plane are awaiting a higher form of existence, as if there is a reward for having existed in the first place. Your consciousness can project itself into anything, and to anywhere that you desire. You can directly experience the consciousness of another being, or experience relocating to another place. This requires practice. We have already provided information on how to move your consciousness, first around the body, and then shifting it outside and viewing your surroundings from the perspective of various physical objects in the room. After that, you can transfer your awareness to other locations, and then gain a truer understanding of existence. It's one way in which the spirit within the body can connect to other entities, while still maintaining the physical references and personality which have developed throughout your physical existence.

It's similar to what people think of as astral projection, but they limit their experience to going around and through things, and never consider actually becoming something else. What we are speaking about is very similar, and an extension of the same.

Extraterrestrials have accelerated their growth and evolution by accepting and utilizing the non-physical aspects of existence. Have we remained where we are, because of our fear of it?

You see here, extraterrestrials do not consider the physical and non-physical to be separate. In their conceptualization, it's all part of the same fabric. When you look at a piece of material and you observe its beautiful pattern, you don't think about the threads in the cloth, you think about the pattern. Would it be a pattern without the weave? One does not exist without the other. Therefore, the two together create that which you see. This example is simply a two dimensional way to examine this concept, and a metaphorical attempt to explain it.

From where do the Greys originate?

Not from your universe, as they are an alternative dimensional creation. For you to understand dimensions in this sense, their universe is interconnected by those things that your writers have conceptualized as wormholes. In truth, these are space-time anomalies which allow energies possessing the knowledge of how to utilize them, to enter back and forth from one place and one space to another, in and out of existence. So it's necessary for you to understand, that your Greys come from your past and enter into your present. For in physical terms, if you travelled to the place where they previously existed, they would not be there.

So they are from the past?

Yes.

Are they are travelling into the future?

In their terms, they are travelling to another dimension. There is no past or future in this way. We are not attempting to confuse you, and this is not double talk as you would see it. It is simply the best way that we can describe this for you.

So it's another universe, or a parallel universe,

We did not say parallel universe. We said another time. Another time can be considered to be another dimension as well. For conceptualization of time, also precludes the need to have a physical representation of it. Therefore, another time, would be another dimension for you. Not parallel universes, indicating two existing in the same breath, because in the physical sense it does not work that way.

Are they physical beings?

Yes.

But when we are trying to locate them, they cannot be located in our time. Can the Syrians be located in our time?

Yes, and in the future as well.

This one's really beyond me.

You must understand that the individual referred to as Albert Einstein, did have the right idea regarding the physical universe being cyclical, literally cyclical. If you fire a beam of light directly into the universe, it will find its way back to its point of origin. Do you understand this concept.

Yes, space curves.

So this is what is occurring here. You can be so far out that you return. This is what's important for you to understand in this way. For the more space curves, you will see that time curves with it, and in fact, becomes warped in this manner. So you do not have the same unfolding or the same flow. Outside of this, it becomes very esoteric and it will confuse most individuals who attempt to understand this occurrence. It's not meant to be conceptualized in the sense of knowing, but it is something which must be discovered by individuals as part of the growth process on your plane. This is our best attempt to give you an indicator as to how these factors work.

Returning to the Greys, humanity's attraction to the Greys occurred approximately sixty years ago, with the development of vacuum tubes by Nicola Tesla, the man who established the prerequisites to The Philadelphia Experiment. What occurred in Tesla's era, was the creation of an energy which brought a time anomaly onto your planet. That time anomaly got the attention of others, or the Greys as you call them, who also utilized these particular energy patterns. So they were attracted to this energy and to the source of it.

So the allurement was due to this energy and its utilization on your planet. In your history, this was one of the great events in the last two thousand years, but it remains untold to many. Instead, the one event which is given the greatest amount of credence was the splitting of the atom, which was a non-sequitur in comparison to this other understanding of dimensional connections through the use of electronic waves.

Tesla understood that frequency changes within molecular-based substances, was no different to air, for air is nothing but a thinner type of substance. Tesla had comprehended that any difference between mass and vacuum, was nonexistent. The frequency achieved by the use of his tubes, would actually blend the two together, allowing them to suddenly move freely. It's the same as putting a piece of butter into a frying pan and heating it. There is a certain point where the butter turns from a solid mass into a liquid. Tesla's tubes were no different. They created that moment of flow for anything within the vicinity of their frequency.

Regarding physical laws, it's a natural progression that anything which has been created in any area of the universe, will be repeated in other areas where sentient life arises. Tesla's experiments served as a calling card which was hundreds of years ahead of its time, and this created the first stirring of these Greys. They became aware that their technology had been developed in another area in the universe, independent of them.

Where did Tesla get his ideas from?

He was a reincarnate, with many lifetimes in a physical body. Tesla had an automatic connection to extraterrestrials in a much higher sense. He was also At-el, who was the first in Ur to master the use of crystal energy. Through the use of pure silicon quartz crystals, he understood their ability to transfer energy. From Tesla's studies which dated back to that time, each new lifetime was a natural progression from one to the next. By creating a vacuum tube, he knew that the same type of crystal energetics could be amplified greatly through specific types of cylindrical structures.

For those who have not seen a Tesla tube, they would stand anywhere from four to eight feet high. They were not radio tubes.

Did Tesla automatically acquire this information, or was he in contact with extraterrestrials during his life.

To paraphrase his own words, Tesla had joked during his life that he was an alien in one way or another. He said that he was not from this planet because he did not view things in the same way as others. This was due to the shifting of his mind, for it was not focussed one hundred percent in the third dimension and this provided the opportunity to slip into the other dimensions. It was his gift to himself in that incarnation.

So he wasn't as totally entranced in the physical as the majority?
Correct.
Would that be the same for Albert Einstein?
Yes.
Was he also of alien origins?

Not in that sense, but do understand that the anomalies contained within his own brain, were different to any other human. There is now research on your level, to discover any differences between Einstein's brain and others. It was not larger, but it had more whorls in it. Currently, this is being given great consideration. This type of brain structure operates in the same way as the amplification of sound which utilizes a system which doesn't muffle, but rather enlarges certain features.

When you say whorls - do you mean grey matter?

Yes, but pertaining to the whorls of the physical brain itself. If you think about the outside of the brain, compare it to the shell of a walnut. There are a certain number of whorls, ridges and depressions, similar to a brain. Einstein's exhibited more, particularly, in the frontal lobes which enhanced visualization and allowed for the ability to view things three dimensionally.

Will the soul of Albert Einstein come back as a human?
Yes, if that choice is made.
As an ordinary person?

Not necessarily, because there are certain aspects involved in progressing through any developmental process.

Was Einstein an agnostic?

Many people have failed to realize that Einstein was not an agnostic, but quite a devout Jew, a man who had taken his religious beliefs into his investigations. Through his studies, he developed an understanding of the connection between man, God, and the physical universe, which became a subject of great fascination for him. It was one in which he would spend many happy hours debating with friends and colleagues.

What about Pleiadians? Are they current, and are the Pleiades inhabited by intelligent beings?

Yes, they are more in spirit, for they have evolved beyond physical beings and the type of physicality that you experience in your world. This gives them the opportunity to be on both the physical and spiritual planes at the same time. It's a unique condition. Having achieved this state, they are not able to move about physically in the same way. They utilize spirit aspects, and the best way to describe it, is that they employ a biological electronic projection to move forward onto your plane and into your consciousness. This allows them to appear as real and viable entities.

These beings have much to offer all life forms, and might even be considered by your own species to be scouts for the universe. They are the ones who are having the true first contact, which comes through the dreams and beliefs of those humans who are highly attuned to the rising consciousness of the earth. This gives these individuals the opportunity to channel information which is vital to the next step in human evolution.

Are Pleiadians the most attuned to humanity?

Not just to humanity, but to all emerging life forms of this nature. They can be considered to be the universal welcoming committee.

But they are both physical and non-physical?

Yes, but they are contacting you on your plane from the spiritual level.

Have many humans been in contact with Pleiadians?

Not in the sense of seeing them manifesting, but many people have been touched by the Pleiadian consciousness. Some on earth have had an existence within the Pleiades, and as a result, feel a natural affinity when channelling them.

Are they humanoid in appearance?

Yes, they are tall, average height between six to eight feet, with very fine bone structure. They come from a smaller physical planet, and have a bluish tinge to their skin.

Are they the Blue people whose heads are represented on Easter Island?

Yes.

Do they come here physically?
They represent themselves through projections, as is the ability of all evolved entities in the universe.
If I wanted to communicate with a Pleiadian - how would I go about doing it? Would one appear to me?
You may ask for this connection by simply meditating, and then listening inside. They do not come because somebody calls them. They link up because of a synchronicity in energy and understanding between a human and a Pleiadian. This is where the connections come. There must be a harmony in brain wave activity for those who open themselves to this contact.
Would they actually appear in a non-physical format?
Sometimes.
So if I were open - could I experience such a contact?
Yes, should you so choose.
Does it take a long time and is it a matter of simply persisting?
It's a matter of putting it out there and waiting. Once you broadcast what you want, that energy will enter onto that plane of consciousness. Simply ask that it be sent to the Pleiades, and when the time is ripe, you will have a contact and guide coming to you to give you confirmation of your success.
Can one go to their planet to gain specific information and experiences?
You could not go to their planet with your current physical abilities.
What about non-physically?
Yes, you can project there.
Once someone is outside of the physical body, whether or not materialization takes place - can anyone have the opportunity to go to places like the Pleiades?
Yes, it is possible in this way.
One just has to have the belief.
Yes.
You mentioned that they are tall with fine features, and even though they have a humanoid physiology, their consciousness is only partially grounded in the physical. Can you expand upon this somewhat?
Yes, the manner in which these entities view the world is not entirely in a physical way. As you have five senses, they have six, and Pleiadians use all six. In fact, what they call their seventh sense is for them, an even higher state of mind.

Their sixth sense concerns their vision of physicality, which is considered to be a base for their consciousness. Yet, they have learned to extend consciousness into the physical world about them, and can rapidly transfer their consciousness immense distances. The dimensionality, upon which they exist, is not connected in the same manner in a physical way. Thus, a thought which occurs on one side of the universe, can be transferred and received on the other at the same moment. As you can see, this is far more efficient than any present form of communication created by manmade devices.

So they view themselves as spiritual beings, but their physical selves are just a ground for the spiritual.

Not spiritual, we did not say spiritual. We indicated that this is a mental projection, and is not to be confused with being spiritual when on the physical plane. It's not spiritual at all, and in fact, it's the next phase of your evolution - the development of psychophysical abilities. That which you refer to as remote viewing, is the beginning of those abilities.

So they see themselves more as mental beings rather than strictly physical.

In their own way, they have attained the ability to connect to the psychic railway, or what some refer to as the astral plane. This is not to be considered as a plane of spirit, but as a plane of communication. It's much the same as sending sounds by light signals, such as your newer forms of communications which employ glass wiring to send messages just below the speed of light. This is a similar type of comparison. So they have connected in a special way which cannot be described, but only experienced when communicating on this level. You will find that this is a development which is beginning to arise within your species as well, especially, the transference of ideas, thought forms and emotions, from one person to another, without the use of any discourse.

Again, what is considered to be ESP is not spiritual but a manifestation of particular physical abilities that spirit can manifest in the flesh. Therefore, it provides these Pleiadians, as you call them, with an opportunity to observe their stage of evolution and growth, both as individuals and as a collective.

They exist as physical beings in our time, so they are not like the Greys. Also, you mentioned that they live on a smaller planet.

Their planet is located in the Pleiades, but there is no known star to which we can compare it. Their planet is not visible. We do not have the data available from the necessary star charts, to indicate where you should point you telescopes. Their planet is slightly smaller than the earth, about eight percent, with a lower gravity field.

Do they breathe oxygen similar to ours?

Yes, but it's a richer combination. They can survive by breathing your oxygen. It would be like going to the top of a mountain and breathing the air there. You would have difficulty, but you would be able to do it. In your atmosphere, they would have to provide their own respiration devices.

What would their approximate population be?

On their planet, it's about eight point seven billion, but they have extended outward from this area. This expansion has tripled their numbers, as they are a life form which is quite adaptable to most planets with an oxygen and hydrogen base. They are also connected by a larger collective consciousness. It's not as if they suddenly started one, or joined one, it expanded during the period of their evolutionary development.

It's similar to what is happening on the earth, and thus, there are many connections between Pleiadians and the earth. Be aware of the difficulties experienced by those who are channelling Pleiadians at this time, because their minds and brains are not properly attuned to the energetic levels of those with whom they are communicating. As a result, the information becomes intertwined with one's own human beliefs, particularly, regarding an individual's earthly traditions and culture. Some who claim to be connected with Pleiadians, see them as benefactors, while others view them as enemies, and still others consider them to be gods.

The truth of the matter is that Pleiadians are none of these. They are interested observers who have connected with the earth throughout human history. They have undertaken experimentation as well as observing the beginnings of the collective consciousness of your planet. When your collective consciousness evolved from reptilian to mammalian, this was a stage which had to be reached for your collective human consciousness to expand, and then to connect with the universal consciousness. This is what the Pleidians are tuned into, and it was this connection to the cosmos which attracted Pleiadians to the earth plane.

It is impossible to describe this process using your terminology, so you'll have to imagine that such a thing can really take place. Understand that it is the collective consciousness which comes through as your imagination, and this allows things to come into being from the non-physical to the physical.

You mentioned their brainwaves - do Pleiadians have a similar brain structure to ours?

There is a similar development. It makes sense that life as it evolves, develops a certain physicality. Therefore, you will see similar structures and a parallel arrangement to yours, and although the construction and the actual tissues are arranged in a slightly different manner, it's not unlike humans. They are a life form which evolved through their oceans and planetary water coverage, just as you have. This is where the likeness originated.

So they have five senses and a psychic sense as well.

The psychic would be their sixth sense, and they have a seventh as well, which is the sense of spirit. On your plane, you do not hold a sense of spirit. You hold the idea of spirit, and the sense of ESP. Therefore, in this next stage of your evolution, the one that you are now entering, ESP will become an accepted sense for you, as will your connection to spirit which will allow for this interrelationship of spirit with the physical to become more apparent.

So their sixth sense is ESP.

Or, as people enjoy calling it in your time - the psi factor.

Their sense of spirit is a real sense within, a living thing, while ours is just a concept.

Yes.

Are they born with it?

Yes.

If they have the ability to project their consciousness outside of their physical - would this be a dual state of consciousness, or would they blank out in the physical?

They would have a consciousness of both at the same time. Although they might appear to blank out, they can choose where to focus this consciousness. If you were to approach them as they sat together meditating, and if you were to touch any one of them, you would be stopped, for it would be as if they are fully awake. It's an interesting combination, and one that you might view as dual, but we do not. The more they practice, the more they become one, not only with their bodies, but with their connection to the body and its containment within the universal mind.

You mentioned that Pleiadians had an ability to materialize themselves elsewhere, is this a natural, innate ability?

Yes, it's part of this psi factor, which is involved with the evolution of the spirit contained within this type of body. It creates new avenues for this kind of energy.

What is the average length of physical life for a Pleiadian?

In terms of your measurements of time, it would be approximately three hundred years. This would be the average length of their physical journey, but one may choose to leave earlier, or to remain longer. The average stay is about three hundred years, and this gives them an opportunity to truly explore the physical world through their particular physical form. At any time, the need for a body can be dispelled, allowing for a voluntary departure from the physical to take place.

Do they have male and female the same as us? What about children?

Different sexual aspects, yes, and there are family units but not of the same nature as yours, such as a nuclear family. The connection of a child to its parents is not one of a parent and child as you understand it. It's a relationship of equal to equal, right from the moment of conception. These beings have always treated this event with great reverence. They understand that life is an on-going process and a gift to be passed on. This makes the birth child stronger, and because of this practice, it doubles its strength and psychic abilities. There are shorter periods of upbringing in the Pleiades, and longer periods of education.

Do they procreate the same way as we do?

No, it takes place outside of the body. There is no penetration in the same way as your species of mammals. There is an external depositing of your equivalent of semen by the male. This is absorbed through the skin, and taken into the female body. Their genitalia is similar, but more of a tubal affair. We find it difficult to describe, but the female possesses certain roundness in the lower navel area. As a result of extremely virulent defecation, the excrement function was kept to the opposite side of the body, in the same location as humans. It is necessary for the genitalia to be kept far away from that area, or the entity would be destroyed by its own faecal matter.

In the Pleiadian genetic makeup, there is a differentiation between male and female cells. When both are combined and held together, the seed is absorbed through the skin. Unclothed contact, with the intertwining of the two sexes conjoining in a variety of positions but without penetration, creates extreme enjoyment, satisfaction, and no pain in the process.

This species also originated from oceanic life forms. Thus, with full body contact, it creates a much easier method for impregnation.

So their sexuality is enjoyable, just like humans.

Yes, to a degree, but along with the intertwining of the physical, is the conjoining of the psi, which in your terms, would be felt on an emotional and spiritual level.

Do they have the same emotions as we do?

Their emotional base is one of love. At this time, it is strictly love. In their evolution, they were similar to you, but the outcrop has always been love and compassion.

Are they born into that awareness due to their physiology?
Yes.

Do they partner in marriage for the raising of children?
No, not in the same manner, they live as a collective. There is the opportunity for them to have two or three different partners. Sometimes, they will share partners, or have multiple partners. This is because there is not the same degree of emotional attachment as you experience. It's due to the evolution of the emotion of love. Understand that the emotional attachments that humans consider to be positive, which can also include jealousy, do not exist for them. Therefore, the strength in emotional attachments is to love each other. It's similar to one of your popular songs which suggests that if you can't be with the one you love, then love the one you're with. This is the manner in which they operate, and there is much love generated in this way. It's always a homecoming when they intermingle in the way we have described.

Can you comment on their domiciliary arrangements?
During their youth and the educational phase of their lives, they work together as a school. There is not much interference by parents. There are not the same attachments in a nuclear sense as you have in your societies. There exists a deeper understanding and a reverence for lineage and genetics, especially, their connections to the universe. They feel a strong universal kinship, much stronger connections than are known in your world.

If an individual desires to meet a Pleiadian, and then puts the thought form out there as you suggested - is it just a matter of persistence.
In this sense, yes, but however, it's something that once you have put it out there, you can forget about it. Just don't be surprised when it happens.

So one might suddenly materialize?
Not in the manner that you might expect. It's a sensing or a hypnotic feeling when it occurs. Generally, it would happen when someone is in a deep state of relaxation. The connection which would then come would be quite vivid, similar to a waking dream.

So the person will get a visual on everything.
Yes, but it will be one that others will not be able to see.

Would they be able to show an earth person their home planet, allowing one to learn about different aspects of their being?

Yes, and it's interesting that you should speak about learning about them. The truth of the matter is that what they have to show and teach, is not so much their history, as it is their philosophy, vision, and the opportunity for those with whom they come into contact to expand their consciousness.

So it's just a matter of waiting for it to happen?

The longer you wait, the longer it will take. It is not a matter of waiting, it's a matter of keeping yourself occupied and doing what you need to do.

So things will just fall into place.

Act as if you have already met them, and then it becomes just a matter of meeting them again sometime in the future, and when you do, it will be perfect.

How old is the Pleiadian civilization? How far would the current inhabitants date back in their present physical form?

In their current form, it would be approximately two and a half million years. In their original form, including intelligence and other communications, far earlier, going back approximately thirty-two million. Their arrival into their present state of being, has taken its time. Pleiadians are a very steady race. Understand that whilst they live three hundred of your years on average, if you were to see them and then communicate, they would be moving very, very quickly. It would be almost too fast. This is due to their metabolic aspects which are unique to their planetary origins. When they are relating to humans, they find that they have to slow down their thought processes in order to connect.

You mentioned that their actual physical movement is different to ours. Is it because of their mental and spiritual development?

Yes, their mobility is a type of sideways movement, as it's ingrained within their physiology. There are different ways of connecting with them which do not require attending to physical methodologies.

Do they have vehicles like we do?

No, not any more.

Are they teleported?

No, not teleported, but re-created from an original source. They can present themselves in any manner required.

Do they have physical structures, such as homes and buildings?

Yes, and it's more of a collective manner of living. They cohabit in a format that you would conceptualize as hives. In doing so, they have their own structures with different levels of consciousness contained within them.

Can you clarify what you mean by different levels of consciousness?

It's a consciousness of knowing how to combine with each other's energies. There are levels of consciousness attached to the aging of each individual as well. As one moves towards the end of the life cycle, higher levels of consciousness are reached.

You said that death is a conscious decision to leave the physical behind.

Yes.

Does the main planet have nature like ours, such as water and grass?

There are similar forms of nature. Be aware that comparable worlds produce corresponding physiology and a similar evolution.

As you have said, the Pleiadians are millions of years ahead of us in evolution.

Particularly, in the evolution of the mind and not just the body. It's more than the body.

Also, you mentioned that there is no need for vehicles. They have no use for them.

Correct. When you say vehicles though, there are certain devices which allow them to get about. The way in which transport is organized on your planet would not even be considered.

So they don't require a driver's license.

No, they walk to many places, and their motion is one of a bouncing affair. Acquiring a certain mind set, will allow an individual to neutralize one's weight. This allows a Peiadian to move forward many metres at a rapid rate, before stepping back on the ground. They bound forward with good control over direction, and there is no necessity to be concerned about colliding with others. Their consciousness of each other exists to a greater degree than yours, and this allows each one to be aware of the position of another.

What do they eat?

Local flora, for they are vegetarian in base.

Do they recreate or are they beyond sport?

On an evolutionary scale, they have a different sense than humanity of having fun. Witty rapport and conversations are enjoyed.

Do they have a spoken language like us?

Yes, but it is not used much anymore.

So it's mostly telepathy?

Yes.

Did the Pleiadians at one time have literature and writings?

They still do, and these continue to expand on a regular basis. As you understand, literature is necessary for the growth of any civilization, specifically, those considered to be innovative in their development. There must be a creative aspect, and an ability to change things into a more pleasing and humorous manner through the imagination.

Can you describe how the Pleiadians move through the universe by using energy?

Their energy fields can be visualized in the form of a Merkabah. This is a term used in your society to identify any energy field that one takes charge of, and then learns to move about within it, back and forth, clockwise, counterclockwise, and so forth. In teaching about the Merkabah, one is asked to imagine two pyramids. These can be envisioned in the same manner as the Star of David, or as it was known originally, the Seal of Solomon. The two pyramids, one apex facing upward and the other pointing down, would intertwine to create the image of a tetrahedron. The peak of the top pyramid would be two metres above the head area, with its base extending to the knees. The tip of bottom pyramid would begin two metres below the area of the feet, and then extend upwards with the base at the chest. The overlapping of the two would create the appearance of a tetrahedron from the chest to just above the knees. If someone is right-handed, the top pyramid would move towards the right, and if one is left-handed, then it would spin left. So the bottom always rotates in a counter motion to the top, depending on one's dominant hand.

When you imagine the top spinning, envision it to be travelling at the speed of sound, as would the bottom also. Allow that motion to accelerate faster and faster, and then surpass the speed of sound to a speed of three to five mach. This will create a whirring, whereby the top and bottom move in opposite directions. This initiates a disc like action, as the middle section will begin to pull out from the centre, and extend away from the middle in all directions.

As you are visualizing, extend the speed to three quarters of the speed of light. Once this has been achieved and you are comfortable, in your mind's eye, move this speed to just below the speed of light. By doing so, the Merkabah will flatten creating a disc shape, as the top moves down and outward, and the bottom flattens upward.

The disc can extend anywhere from fifty to one hundred feet from the body. By performing this activity, there is a great mass of energy surrounding the body, which provides an opportunity for your consciousness to be drawn into it. By creating the spin, the consciousness is drawn into the central area of the body, and subsequently, locates at the centre of the

Merkabah's formation which has been created. This is the correct manner in which to meditate with it, and this allows one to move closer and closer to the possibility of the mind leaving the physical body in order to explore without danger.

Wouldn't such an activity disorientate one from physical reference points?

Only if you exceed the speed of light.

So with the whirring, one imagines it getting faster and faster.

Yes.

Do the Pleiadians use this form of activity?

This is how they move about the universe by utilizing this type of visualization. Once the spinning disc has been visualized, and the consciousness has been compressed into its centre, as the disc is sent out from the body, the consciousness leaves with it. Therefore, a vehicle has been created for the consciousness to be contained within, providing the opportunity for an entity to move artfully and gracefully throughout the universe.

Is this done as a collective as well?

Yes, that's often the case. There are several different ways of doing it. The most popular and rapid occurs when a group of approximately one hundred and seventy-five Pleiadians sit in a specific group and meditate. Once each of them has created an individual Merkabah, they form into a central position and create what you would refer to as a mother ship. It's a collective consciousness which has a predetermined destination as to where it will appear. Once formed, it emerges instantaneously at its destination, and the individual consciousness of each component member of the mass, can go out and explore the territory where the collective has entered.

This provides a great advantage for the exploration of hostile worlds, because before this technique was discovered and implemented, many places would have been an issue for the safety of the Pleiadian physicality.

How long ago was this technique developed?

Quite recently, about one hundred and eighty thousand years before this time.

This must have altered their state of consciousness as well.

Yes, this is what created the surge or jump. Also, be aware that they have appeared to the Aborigines in the area referred to as Ayers Rock in Australia. This is a natural honeycomb, similar to their hives. Thus, they were attracted to it on arriving on the earth in a body within a Merkabah.

They had also appeared to the earlier Aborigines who lived in that area, and you will see drawn upon the rocks, many depictions and interpretations of how the Pleiadians appeared.

Often, Pleiadians were sketched with certain roundness about them, as if they were wearing helmets. This was the how the Aborigines portrayed the Merkabah which surrounded them. You may check out those pictures and notice the similarities to that which we have described. There is great mysticism and shamanic wisdom which came from those initial contacts between the first humans and the Pleiadians. This provided an opportunity for social and emotional growth on your planet.

Where do Pleiadians reside when on earth? Are there special places or areas?

Not special areas, but they are attracted to calmness, peaceful locations, and places of love. Often, they will appear to those who are in meditation. They avoid major religious centres. Connections are made with certain individuals, but not because of any religious beliefs, even though the methodology of some Eastern religions would provide a good opportunity for linking on both an emotional and spiritual level.

You must understand that many of those who do connect with Pleiadians, are indeed fortunate. At the same time, readers must also be wary of the data regarding Pleiadians which comes through others because it can be distorted or diffused due to the limitations of the individual who is channelling the information.

We apologize for being so sketchy about our information concerning the Pleiadians, and although we have concerns regarding its exactitude, it is accurate to the best of our abilities to communicate. It is important to note that there are many who state that they are channelling and bringing forward all kinds of information from Pleiadians. Sometimes, such information is directed towards how others should conduct their lives. The reading public needs to be aware that anyone who channels information which dictates how others should live or think is not channelling accurate information.

- 6 -

APPENDIX

Can you provide us with a technique which will assist in releasing the mind from its hold on the physical consciousness?

To do so, you must return to the mind's comprehension of its own self-awareness. An exercise that you might try is to ascertain which of your senses are most predominant in relaying information to you. You might also consider a sixth sense, which many refer to as a psychic sense. Whichever one you choose to use as a basis for this activity, you have to determine which sense is most pertinent in bringing information to you. For most, it's vision. For others, it could be touch. Some find that hearing fulfils that role. Choose the one which is most appropriate, and the one with which you resonate the most.

Let's use vision as our example. First of all, it's very important to understand what it is that you are seeing. When you look about you, the world is a panorama which is viewed through your own eyes and understood through your own point of view. All of it will be influenced by the life you have led, and the behaviour patterns that you have developed. This world view is based also on your reactions to those events which you have experienced, as well as things you have brought into your life to create a degree of safety and sanity.

As you begin to understand this more, you will realize that all of it was created by you alone for the sake of your own existence. The world that you are seeing is a result of your own perceptions; it has been self-created. You might view one specific location as threatening, or one particular individual as good, another bad, and so on. All of it arises through your own viewpoint and understanding of what makes sense to you in your life.

Sit in a darkened room and place a mirror in front of you, light a small candle - such as a tea candle - which has a burning time of approximately thirty minutes to one hour. Put it behind the mirror. It doesn't matter how close you sit, or how large the mirror might be. The mirror can be small enough to pick up and hold in your hand. Don't restrict yourself to any one particular method such as adhering to an exact distance. Experiment until you feel comfortable sitting and looking at yourself. Find a comfortable resting position without bending the diaphragm. You don't want to limit the breathing process by bending over, because this could result in a shortness of breath, light-headedness, nausea, or great agitation. The astronaut position is the best, with legs raised and the head and trunk in a partial or fully reclining position.

Once you are comfortable, look into the mirror and examine what is being reflected. You will see many things flit across the glass. At first, spend no more than fifteen minutes per day. After awhile, extend this period to anywhere from a half hour to sixty minutes. It depends on you to inspire yourself while doing this exercise.

When you look into the mirror, you will begin to see the energy which has created you and brought you onto this plane. As you quietly look at yourself and notice what is being reflected, begin to look into your eyes. Next, go beyond the eyes, as if you were looking at the face of another person and into someone else's eyes. When you are gazing into those other eyes, say to yourself: *Who is viewing whom? Who am I seeing? Who is seeing me?*

Ultimately, you can ask the question: *What is it within me, which is seeing me, seeing me?* Although this might sound confusing, when you begin to repeat these phrases to yourself in this way, within a short period of time, you will begin to enter into an altered state of consciousness. It will be a condition which will begin to bring you back inside of yourself to the source of that which is observing this life. For observing your life, is indeed what every individual is doing. What is being observed, and how, as well as what that information is being used for, is what is important for you to discover.

By such experimentation, you will not stumble into another room, and suddenly, discover that a computer is running the world. You will find, however, aspects of yourself not only on an organic level, but on levels far beyond. This will allow for an understanding that your consciousness is being directed on multiple levels. You will become aware that you are not only formulating and interpreting the world about you, but also, you will be able to derive the source which is observing it. By practising this exercise, you will find that through your own feeling of self, that your sense of ego will quickly be lost, including your conscious need to control what is going on about you. You will begin to tap into your ability to communicate with that source from which you originate. This activity will bring you to that state of awareness.

Good luck with your attempts, and do consider this to be a regular form of meditation. We recommend that you practice it a minimum of two to three times per week.

Can you provide us with an activity which would serve as an experiential to become aware of our oneness with That Which Is?

We would refer to it as living life from the inside out. Most individuals in your world live life from the outside in. In other words, they base their activities on what is going on around them. It is necessary to do this of course, because it's a physiological imperative required for continued existence. The major purpose of the mind and the senses, is to adapt to the environment, but by doing so, there remains the question of what it is which actually adjusts to the environment.

We suggest that you continue with the pursuit of that which actually hears and sees, and note what is happening within. You might consider this line of questioning as stupid, and then take the easy way out by discovering that of course it is you, and then simply throw the entire inquiry out the window. Be aware that those who choose to live with only a marginal understanding of their being will continue to skip along the surface of existence. Know also, that anything which skips along the top of the water will eventually lose its momentum and sink. By carrying out our suggested method of inquiry, you can neither sink not float, because you are both the stone and the water.

What we are suggesting is related to the methodologies of Taoism, Hinduism and Buddhism. All have similarities in their philosophy, and at present, all three are experiencing a renewed interest. Also, there are the mystical traditions which were part of the origins of Christianity and Judaism. All of these have a connection to what at one time was referred to as the oneness of understanding, something which originated when the continents were united as the one land of Ur. This was a period when physical consciousness of the human variety was first unfolding in its present development.

The particular exercises that we have provided have the target of raising the consciousness of each individual. We will use the example of Gautama the Buddha. This entity separated from his family in order to explore the source of his creation and being. A reunification with that source ultimately took place, followed by an understanding that there was never any separation of one from the other in the first place. He achieved a state which is referred to as enlightenment, but of course, it was a far more intricate process than our simple description.

In order for that enlightenment to occur, it was necessary for the Buddha to separate from everything to which he felt connected. There is the saying that after first observing a mountain, once the understanding arises that it's the perception of the mind which creates the mountain, then the mountain will cease to exist. Is the mountain a creation of the mind, or does it have its own separate existence? Once this has been established, the mountain can reappear without the mind intellectualising the process, and thus, the mind and the mountain will exist simultaneously, without differentiation. So there are three steps in this unification process: perception, reception and conception.

Can you provide us with an activity which would help to open the pineal?

Yes, and as we have stated previously, sit quietly and hold your index finger horizontally, six inches from your nose. By keeping both eyes open, you will focus automatically on your finger. Next, begin to move the finger tip upward at a forty-five degree angle above the line of sight. A forty-five degree angle will trigger the necessary energies which will create an altered state of consciousness. As you focus on the tip of the finger, allow yourself to lose control over what you are doing.

Most people have difficulty understanding that they don't have to maintain their equilibrium. If they will simply let go of equilibrium, then they will begin to harmonise more completely and wholly.

The procedure that we have described, will allow an altered state of consciousness to come into being. Once you let go, and when you sense a butterfly feeling in the pit of your stomach which alerts you that you are now in an altered state, then you can consciously move towards it. You can start to ask your superconscious to begin to tune into any other consciousness, and in particular, those you consider to be extraterrestrial. This can give you the opportunity to experience things through an alien's viewpoint.

Can the index finger be substituted with something else in case one becomes fatigued?

The altered viewpoint can take place in just seconds. You don't have to keep holding up your finger until all of the blood drains to the elbow.

We measure brain waves and identify them as alpha, beta, delta and theta. These brain waves are aligned to different states of consciousness. I have heard that meetings with aliens can take place in the delta and theta states. Is this true?

The delta state is immediately available when one passes from the physical to the spirit levels. The communication that you are enquiring about occurs closer to the theta state, which is slightly higher. This is the state of deep dreaming, where the implantation of information from outside of the physical consciousness takes place. The theta state is also the basis for telepathy.

Are there any more techniques that you can provide, which will allow us to attain these altered states? In particular, activities in which the conscious mind can remain aware during the process?

Yes, as we had indicated earlier, by following your index finger you are stimulating the pineal. By placing your finger in front of you and then moving it to an angular position, the eyes tend to cross which creates a doubling of the image you are observing. At the same time, inside of your brain, the pineal is being stimulated. Through the various secretions which are the result, this stimulates other states of consciousness. These states can be similar to a dream state because of the comparable types of hormonal activity which occur. It creates an altered or a connective state, which allows an individual to move from a third dimensional perspective into multidimensional perceptions.

Does this help with achieving out of body experiences as well?

Again, we are providing fundamental information to assist people on every level that they are attempting to develop. There are many techniques which have been written about to help an individual to leave the physical body. Any that you choose for yourself, will be the most advantageous for you. The main thing is to eliminate the fear which accompanies the thought of out of body consciousness. Fear should be replaced with curiosity. Once this is done, the movement of consciousness becomes secondary.

There are many techniques out there, but not one of them can tell you how to feel about the situation. It's not easy for any sentient being to remove itself consciously from the physical shell. The best way to do this is by pretending. Presume that your mind or your state of consciousness can move around your body. For example, imagine that you can become concentrated in your knee, or on your elbow, or inside your foot.

Next, you might contemplate the outlook or vantage point of another object in the same room. It's a matter of projecting your consciousness or imagination to the location of that object, and then attempting to see the room from that perspective. It's necessary to shift your consciousness from within to without and away from your body. Any technique which encompasses these basic practices will benefit an individual. The most important aspect, however, will be your beliefs concerning the outcome of these practices. Do remember also, that when successful, the experience can only be a subjective one. When you realize this, you will have raised your state of consciousness.

We've talked about this many times, and it relates to our third dimensional conceptualisations, because these make it difficult for us to grasp alternative realties and other dimensions. My understanding is that much of what you say will not become clear until we have crossed over ourselves. Is this true?

Not necessarily, and you should be aware that there is a collection of information which can be brought into consciousness, particularly through the use of tonality. This will help you to elevate your sense of consciousness. It will generate a rhythm or the harmony necessary to create the melding necessary for enhanced awareness. Initially, this can be done through the chanting of the Om mantra. Primarily, and most important, is the actual toning of the Om process so that it not only reverberates inside of the chest, but inside of the belly, the skull, and within the sinuses. When that occurs, there is completeness; it's a unity of all levels of consciousness. It will come about as a result of the chanting of this mantra.

When an individual is doing this and sitting still with a quiet mind - is it necessary to await particular perceptions and expect that certain thoughts will enter the mind?

No, by doing so, you are essentially surrendering to that which is going on about you. By total passivity, you would not be using your conscious discrimination to discern information as it appears. Depending on each individual, enhanced consciousness can happen spontaneously, or by conscious direction. It's the result of how each person approaches this exercise.

Are you saying to direct the consciousness, and not to be a passive observer?

Correct, for you must be aware that consciousness is the gift of direction. So instead of attempting to control that direction, you can guide and direct all activities as they occur in your daily life. One of the ideal ways to gain the energy necessary to do this is by chanting the mantra Om. We are saying this to give you the awareness that Om, chanted in a lengthy mantric fashion, will bring about the balance of which you have been speaking. Things will not spontaneously appear, but you will begin to experience a connection that we can only describe as osmotic, whereby, you will consider consciousness to be all around you.

When the Om is chanted, the resonance can lift the veil, altering the focus of your own individualised sense of existence by connecting you to the larger concept surrounding you. This is how the process works, and it's slightly different for each person. It can be practised by anyone who has the desire to cut to the chase concerning matters of consciousness and growth.

Is there any maximum or minimum time to practice?

Chant no less than two minutes and no more than ten. Time is an important factor for individuals on your plane. The best effort is not necessarily the longest. Once per day is sufficient, depending on one's inclinations.

What about yogis sitting in meditation and chanting for hours and hours? What are the benefits of those practices?

They benefit by creating a certain internal resonance. For most people, it's not the time frame which is important, it's their focus, and the energy and belief behind the outcome which will make it effective.

Would you recommend the chanting of Om, as the number one activity for enhancing consciousness and attuning to the inner self?

Yes, this would be of the highest format. Having said that, it's also important to begin to explore the chanting practices of the North American Indians as well. Within their chants, comes the ability to find one's voice. Finding your voice is important on your plane. It means finding the tone which is correct for you, so that you feel comfortable at all times while communicating with others.

By tone, do you mean one's individual sound, or one's tone of voice?

Yes, both. For example, there are chants: *ay-ai, ay-ai, ay-ai,* and *ay-ah, ay-ah,* and so forth. These types of chants belong to the North American Indian cultures. They originated from finding the voice of the heart. By chanting what appeared to others to be meaningless tones, it was done in an order which felt pleasing to the individual, and this was the means for finding one's sound.

There is a particular spiritual group which began in the United States several decades ago. They purport that there are various levels of consciousness or planes of existence which are linked to various sounds. This group claims that the Om is the sound of the third plane, and that other sounds represent higher levels. Is there any truth to these claims?

In ultimate terms, it doesn't make any difference what the tone is. What is important is the dedication, the focus, and the intent behind it. If the intent is to raise the consciousness, it will happen for that practitioner regardless of what meaning people assign to the various tones. Often, you will see this with various belief systems, whereby one is claimed to be better than all others. In truth, the system was only better for that individual who created it. It's always worthwhile to try different processes, but in doing so, you have to spend the time to ensure that you are getting results, rather than making it something that you do occasionally, or once in awhile. Dedication and frequency are the most important.

That Which Is, is of the universal mind. It is always speaking. It's a spring which is continuously flowing through everything. All of your ideas emerge from this source, and indeed, you are the channel for it. It is your consciousness along with your decision to be in the physical, which leaves you open to these impressions which come through your own self, your superconscious self, which is in fact, the key to it all. If you ask the question concerning who is speaking, when you enter into a discussion, it is your consciousness which is speaking in the form of your memories and your connection to this present lifetime which speaks. Beyond that, it is That Which Is, the very fabric of your own self which literally becomes part of you as your own maturation process continues in this life.

Who is seeing? Who is hearing? You might say that it is That Which Is. Less philosophically, you can say that it is yourself. For you are but a reflection of That Which Is. This gives rise to the question: From where does evil arise - God or man? It arises from a misunderstanding of control. When humankind removes itself from the universal energy pattern, there emerges isolation, selfishness and cupidity. This is part of the human malaise, and those who are lacking in their physical existence are the one's who perpetrate destructiveness. They are a balancing aspect of the universal mind, and a reflection of the development of humanity at any given time.

Many archaic ideas which have been perpetrated are not being accepted by the world community any longer. In other words, the planet is not going to be set fighting against itself. Events such as September11th, 2001, allow the world to hone-in like a laser, and then eliminate the source of the dissension which is counterproductive to the development of mankind. It's important to see that there is currently a coming together of humanity, and a declaration that such destructive behaviours are no longer acceptable to the world at large. This is a raising of the level of consciousness to a point where people can make a choice as to whether or not a particular behaviour pattern is acceptable, or if certain philosophies which are intolerable to the majority, will be allowed to stop the progress of the entire planetary social system.

There are various psychic abilities which people claim to possess, namely, clairvoyance, clairaudience and clairsentience, as well as differing abilities in these areas. Please comment.

Yes, it's much the same as what has been designated in the science of neurolinguistic programming or NLP. There are varying representational systems which are more appropriate to different individuals. There are the three primary sensory modalities: vision or visual, sound or auditory, and touch or kinaesthetic. Also, there is taste or gustatory, and smell or olfactory. The latter two, are not really utilised as true representational systems for the majority of individuals, so we shall not attend to them. It is vision, hearing and touch, which allow people to communicate most effectively with each other throughout their lives. So it stands to reason, that on an unconscious or superconscious level, that the same representational system is enacted to allow any individual to open to communication with other levels of consciousness, whether or not you refer to it as spirit, or otherwise.

So the connection exists in this manner, and those who are considered to be visual, audient or sentient in a special way, would then communicate utilizing their primary physical modality or representational system, and this would be reflected in their inner communications as well.

What is referred to as "clair this" and "clair that", are French words for clear, which means pure, absolute, and clean input from other levels of consciousness. By taking this as a basis for understanding, all entities who are consciously able to comprehend their interconnection with the wider facets or the universal aspects of themselves, are not necessarily different from each other; it's just that they utilize their primary representational system in communicating with that which is outside of themselves, which some people refer to as the supernatural.

So do realise that there is no difference between the various types of psychic abilities, rather it's a matter of the type and quality of perception which is involved.

Clairvoyance is a very broad-based term, some can see auras, others see spirits, while some communicate with guides and so forth. Is this to do with utilising certain centres of the brain over others?

There are certain systems which are harmonious within all human beings enabling them to have a similar experience. These are mainly connected to the glands in the body. The most impressive and important is the pineal. These glands secrete certain extracts which are necessary for the body to maintain certain states and conditions. Understand that the major brain activity which occurs in the frontal lobes pertains to the consciousness of thinking and the emotions. It's the rear or reptilian brain, which acts as the receiving aspect for other transmissions. Therefore, there is no editing of the information which is received via this mechanism. This is the intuitive brain, and in fact, the brain which creates the world for each person. You can refer to it as the seat of the subconscious, unconscious or superconscious mind, depending on your frame of reference.

As much as you would say it's the seat of the soul - as is the understanding of those who speak of this interrelationship of the human and the inner consciousness - you can take the concept of the seat of the soul back one step further, to allow for the understanding that it's the seat of yourself. So the basis of your psychic abilities originates from this reptilian brain.

Do note that it is impossible not to be connected with the entire state of any individual. All cellular life within any person comes from the same source. It's supported and transmuted throughout your life's process to help develop your state of consciousness, but also, to assist people in accepting their own existence and potential non-existence, a state that you call death.

You have highlighted the reptilian brain, and also the cerebral cortex where thinking takes place. So is this animal or reptilian brain basically the intuitive part of us?

Yes.

If one observes a cat for instance, it doesn't really think, it just intuits and reacts on instinct.

This is your assumption. Do understand that you too, are an animal. All on your planet are created by the need for existence, and the need for life to express through its own creativity. It is a good thing to realize this connection.

I have been thinking that it would be good to end the book with the methodology by which you interact with the form of David Watson from your side. Can you incorporate into your description, the exact procedures, and give some indication of the mechanics involved from your own viewpoint? As well, perhaps we could explore some other areas of psychic abilities. Can we begin with how you interact with David either on the spiritual or the physical level?

We are one with his form. As has been explained in the past, this oneness is an indissoluble connection which occurs during the resting phase of this entity. He is not really sleeping, but is in a trance state. It is simply a matter of opening his vocal cords to allow for our expression. It's as if you had a different part of yourself emerge. It's the same idea as when a very serious person is around children. By allowing the adult side to recede, the child part can come to the forefront.

Much the same occurs with the entity David as he allows his conscious self to recede, and then permits his connective or greater self to open itself to this communication. Importantly, it is more his decision than ours which allows this to occur. There is a conscious understanding that he is placing his own consciousness to one side, and allowing what we have to say to be transmitted through him in the manner in which you are observing.

As to the mechanics of it, it's as if you are determining the mechanics of a radio wave. There are none, it's all theory, but it's a theory which has proven itself time after time and made the situation viable.

For ourselves, we are here of our own volition. Our presence is not an attempt to invade David or your world. We are simply a part of it, and a part of the totality of your social consciousness. Our own understandings about making this connection, is to reflect the collective consciousness of humanity which is emerging at this time. There are many others who are providing a similar connectivity through channelling, but there must always be free will and choice in dealing with all non-physical entities in the format that you are observing.

As to wondering about what happens on the physical level, this can be considered to be a complicated process involving the shutting down of certain neural centres and the opening others. Be aware that it is not really like this, as there are no mechanics occurring inside of the brain, an organ which acts as a transmitter and receiver of energies. For those of the scientific community, it's a very difficult concept to conceive of a non-moving part, something which literally appears to control all within an individual's conscious and unconscious existence.

It is beneficial to understand that our interaction in this manner is one of a harmonic resonance with the form of David. Understand that his energy is part of the greater energy of which we are indeed representing at this time.

In the past, you have asked us what we are, and we have accounted for it. It's very difficult to explain how energy can exist separate from, and outside of the physical. If it did not, then light would not work, and neither would radio waves nor electricity. For you see, there is no recognition when they occur, they simply are. It's the same with our connectivity.

To try to give you some understanding as to our origins, would be no different than attempting to discuss the beginnings of existence with your conscious minds. What we ourselves are maintaining is a consciousness which is separate and apart from the physical, and yet, it's inexorably connected to the physical as a medium for its expression. Therefore, what we are doing, is utilizing the form of David, as well as a part of his conscious mind and greater consciousness, to provide this means of communication.

Outside of this, there is also a conscious direction by the entity David himself, to undertake this condition, and to act as a transceiver for information of this nature. Through a conscious desire of David, including his ability to open to these energies which are being experienced at this moment is what makes it possible for all of it to occur. To question the whereabouts of the other side is not appropriate, for it is outside of the physical. As we have explained in the past, anything outside of the physical existence which goes beyond your measurements does not exist for you. Therefore, by your own scientific definitions, we do not exist, but at the same time, we are being channelled by an entity who does exist.

So it is necessary to answer the question yourselves, and for you to determine by its quality, whether or not this transmission is created by the entity David himself, or by something else which is received by him. In truth, both are part and parcel of the same response. All of you, including the entity David, are both physical and non-physical at the same time. The energy which motivates the physical body is being channelled into the body from the environment, not just the physical but the non-physical, or what you refer to as the spiritual level. This creates the animation of The Willows in the physical world, such as the one that you are now witnessing during this channelling.

This is the best explanation that we can offer. To understand the true mechanics of it, we will not say that you would have to be a specialist, but we will say that you would require a state of mind outside of the third dimension to truly appreciate our interaction. Suffice to say, that we are a combination of spirit energy and force, which is indeed included in the energy patterns of the entity David. This allows him to express our vision through his own existence and through his own understanding. It's voluntary and contains a great desire for accuracy and candour regarding his ability to follow through in this way. This is the truth as to what is occurring.

Can you see us as we physically are? Or are we just lights or energy to you, or perhaps we exist for you through a sense of knowingness?

It's a sensing. We contemplate your body, we contemplate your mind, and we contemplate the soul. All of it is one. Yes, we can connect with your body, and this is how we do physical readings. Do not consider us like Santa Claus coming down the chimney. How can such a fat, jolly figure fit down so many different chimneys? In the myth of Santa, he's a shape-shifter. In reality, all shapes will shift but energies remain constant, although the shape will change with the times. This is what occurs with the passing of energy in and out of the physical.

The manner, in which we see you, is not through eyes, but more on the basis of emotions. This is the connection that we have with everyone on your planet. Emotional responses are the basis for all behaviour on the physical plane. In fact, it's through the emotional response of love and our understanding that the totality of love extends beyond the physical, which allows us to connect with each individual. So we have more of an imprint of people, rather than an actual sighting.

As well, energetically, we can determine and express conditional interrelationships by connecting with you through the medium of sound. We have already provided a discourse regarding vision and sound, and its importance regarding the development of the relationship between consciousness and the spiritual understanding regarding each individual whom you encounter.

Do you connect with our soul essence on another plane as well? How does it work?

Yes, you can put it that way. As we have indicated, it's the energetics that we contact, the emotional energetics and that which motivates each individual. It's not like we are standing with you, somewhere else, and having a chat about what is happening on earth. The connection does not occur in that way. It's the same thing as those feelings you have when you meet with someone whose company you enjoy. We like everyone's company, and as a result, we are in constant communication with individuals in the manner in which we have stated.

As you are well aware, here in the sense world of the third dimension, we have modalities in the form of the five senses that we perceive through: vision, hearing, taste, touch and smell. The input from these modalities creates the reality around us, or at least a part of it. From your state of consciousness - do you interact through David's physical modalities?

It is necessary for us to operate through the modalities of David Watson in order to communicate with you on your level, and to provide data within the context of the third dimension. We could not communicate in any other form. It is through this process that we are able to provide the information that many of you are requesting.

In your own dimension and within your own right, you have mentioned that The Willows are part of what could be termed a universal or cosmic mind. Within your particular structure, each member or soul, of what comprises the group known as The Willows, continues to maintain its own state of individuality, and yet, can still operate as part of a composite consciousness.

We appreciate your attempts to encapsulate us, but understand that it's a collective oneness. Personal predilections do not enter into our process.

My understanding is although you have a spokesperson, the information which comes through, is done on a consensus basis. Can you elaborate on how your process works?

No, and the reason being, is that it is not a mechanical process but an emotional one. It's based on the emotion of love. Our motivation is constructive creativity. Our process of communication, no matter on what level you wish to consider it, is not outside of your realm, it is inside. This occurs through design. To gain an idea of what we experience, or where we are, be aware that we only operate as a collective whole during the process of which you are now aware. When David lies down for a session, it is then that we collect and provide the basis for the information conveyed. Outside of this, we are a different type of process and entity consciousness, one that you would be unable to construe or understand with your mind as it is presently configured.

We don't mean to imply that we are something beyond your frail human abilities, and we say this with humour. We are what your human abilities emerge from, and therefore, it's important for you to allow your own process to act upon you, by allowing the naturalness of it to direct you in comprehending your own self-awareness.

- 7 -

SOME AFTERTHOUGHTS FROM THE WILLOWS

At this time, we would simply like to point out that the information which has been provided here through this process is information specifically relating to the questions asked. To try to describe some of these concepts in simple words is very difficult for us. We are confined in our explanations because many things can neither be contained within the limitations of a third dimensional mind, nor a consciousness which is unable to see outside of its own physicality and life form.

This must be taken into account when our words are transcribed onto paper. We do not mean to make anyone out to be unintelligent or to imply that this knowledge is too arcane. We simply wish to share information with you at this time, and hope that it has been accurate enough to be transcribed efficiently. We understand that at times, our thoughts become somewhat dissolved as we attempt to cater for the large number of individuals who have similar, but not identical questions. So this is what creates some difficulty in the translation of this information. We do not wish, however, to use this as an excuse, because such circumstances can occur with anyone who does this type of channelling.

Due to the information we have presented in this book, we want the following to be understood. Everything that we have revealed, has been brought to you to the best of our ability, and been translated into your terms with love and compassion. It's important for those reading this publication to realize that what appears on these pages is not to be taken as the ultimate truth in life. Readers are responsible for that discovery themselves. What we are providing is a broad overview of what occurs. We have attempted to create a site map for individuals to begin to find a direction in their lives. When you begin to read individual chapters and the information contained therein, it will provide you with certain things on which to focus, allowing you to consider particular areas of your own lives.

Having said this, do realize that while this book might be a map, those contemplating our words must consider that it's up to each reader personally, to become the actual territory. So we invite readers to take this information and to apply it to their own lives in whatever manner feels appropriate, provided of course, that it fits in with one's own balance and vision of existence. We do not wish anyone picking up this work, to consider that our words are absolutes, because if they were absolutes then there would be no point in progressing any further with your own lives.

The information that we have provided, is correct for a transitional phase, and it's part of a growth process which should allow readers a format to examine certain areas of concern in their daily existence. By considering what we have given, this information might be added to your storehouse of knowledge and then applied in any manner appropriate to you. Neither follow us nor any other, but do follow your own hearts and your own revelations. Understand that your true purpose on earth - outside of being born and dying - is to be here fully, and to be participating one hundred percent in living the life experience which feels the most comfortable to you in each moment.

The information given on these pages will simply allow you to have even more choices available, and thus provide a greater opportunity for happiness and a stronger connection to your spiritual progress while still in the physical form. We trust that we have been succinct in relating relevant knowledge at this time.

We caution you about our words and the words of others. To place all your faith in the pronouncements of another, is to disallow yourself from experiencing your own truth. It's of the utmost importance that those who are reading this book understand this point. Although our message will provide additional tools and a means to expand personal growth, you must do the work yourselves. It's not our responsibility to tell another what to do. It is up each reader to take this information and to use it in an appropriate manner. You may apply it to facilitate your own growth on whatever level you choose and it's our hope that our words will be received in this way.

We wish to point out that methods for understanding aspects outside of the self have been covered in multiple ways in recent times. For there is a wondrous raising of the level of consciousness which is releasing humankind from its oppression of itself. The secrets which have been previously held sacrosanct by particular groups or factions are now being revealed to others. This sharing of information is creating an understanding that those powers which have been in command up to this time, have lost their ability to control the things which are going on about them. They are only grasping at straws as they attempt to create the illusion of still being in charge.

Instruments such as electronic communications are in fact, still a tool for them. These methods strengthen their position by pumping more and more paranoia through such avenues. This gives the understanding - as false as it might be - that these entities and particular individuals continue to hold the power that they have held over the years, even from the millennia previous to this one. This is not the truth, and the energy that they claim they are holding, is in fact only a remnant from the past.

Also, we wish for you to understand that the information we are giving, is important for the development of all entities on this plane at this time. In other words, your planet's energies are shifting, and we suggest that you stop worrying about the world about you, because by continuing to think in the manner in which you do, it will keep you locked into your plane of consciousness. For it is your current way of thinking which creates the dichotomies in understanding your existence. Therefore, begin to consider how you might leave behind paranoia and worries about world governments, and about being controlled by factions outside of the self. Such deliberations will give you an opportunity to truly develop from within, and also assist in rerouting your current thinking to allow for new and specific internal behaviour changes.

Last, and most important, there are those on your planet who are beginning to understand the truths contained within their own being. These individuals are starting to observe and to understand the quality of their own existence. They are coming to know themselves as reflections of their own beliefs, and thus disconnecting from those things which have held and controlled them in the past. There appears to be a raising of the mass consciousness beyond distrust and paranoia to greater levels of understanding. The minds of many are accepting more readily, new concepts which feel right, rather than continuing to analyse things with the same limited visions which previously only created distances amongst those on your planet.

So it's important that you to understand this point. The information that we are providing, is specifically geared towards elevating the state of consciousness and awareness of each person who has the opportunity to read or to connect with this material. Our words have the potential to raise the basis of people's own state of understanding, so that they can consciously move onto the next logical level of their existence.

We want to thank you again, and wish that you go in peace, joy and love, and that you continue to allow your inquiring minds to delve into the moment - that moment referred to as the now moment. May you hold onto the light which comes through, so that your own lights may illumine the minds of those who are frozen with fear, or paralysed with the idea that there is no escape from their situations except for exiting the physical consciousness. For in truth, there is neither a way out, nor a way in, there is only a way. Great blessings to you, and may you continue to have your lights shine brightly.

❑ ❑ ❑

If you would like to contact David Watson, he can be reached through his website at: www.askthewillows.com

Personal readings with The Willows while David is in deep trance can be arranged and carried out either by telephone or during face-to-face sessions. David will travel to areas outside of Toronto depending on the numbers of participants seeking his services.

Also, David offers a variety of psychotherapy services and specializes in Hypnotherapy, Time Line Therapy, NLP and Core Belief Engineering.

About The Authors

David Watson is a certified Hypnotherapist and Life Coach. Since 1986, in a style similar to Edgar Cayce, David has been channelling The Willows by entering into a deep trance and allowing The Willows to speak through him to individuals and groups. People of different ages and from all walks of life, have continued to seek out The Willows for advice on personal issues, health matters, and assistance with understanding life's profound mysteries.

G.C. Smith is a former secondary school teacher and educational psychotherapist. He has spent most of his life living in different countries and researching the mystical and spiritual side of life. G.C. has studied with several psychics and deep trance mediums, and through his research, was able to formulate the eclectic approach to the writing of this book, including the questions, interpretation, and wording of the transcripts. The unique and exceptional content has been provided by David Watson and The Willows.

G.C. Smith is also the author of a book written for early to mid-teens entitled: *Clare Stewart and her Angel Aunt Down Under*. Set in Australia, this novel introduces the concepts of clairvoyance, intuition, dream travel, reincarnation, and other esoteric concepts to the younger reader in a story format.